THE
WORLD
IN
FOCUS

THE WORLD IN FOCUS

Foreword by Alan Whicker

Text by Roger Hicks

COLOUR LIBRARY BOOKS

CLB 2026
© 1988 Colour Library Books Ltd., Guildford, Surrey
Printed and bound in Barcelona, Spain by Cronion, S.A.
All rights reserved
ISBN 0 86283 610 7
COLOUR LIBRARY BOOKS

Foreword
By Alan Whicker

Whicker's World has been turning on television for around 30 years, and I am hoping that all those far-flung programmes have encouraged you to watch – and then to get up and go! Such documentaries seek to offer a new outlook, to open a window on the world, to show what lies waiting for you over the hill... It could be something wonderful.

Scenery is not doing anything – it's just lying there looking lovely; yet like a beautiful woman or a splendid meal, it proffers repletion, promises deep satisfaction. To be lucky enough to see Lake Atitlán among its volcanoes or Norfolk Island in its blue Pacific, the Taj Mahal at dawn or Manhattan at twilight – such sights last a lifetime. Kashmir or Milford Sound or Bali or any of the glorious scenes you are about to consider within offer us a holiday for the eyes and the senses, and a good reason for living.

Even when the difference between one superb landscape and another is not great, there is always a world of difference between the people who look at it: in an early Whicker's World one splendid Boston matriarch set me aback by declaring "Why should I travel when I'm already *here*?" She was standing at the far end of my personal scale of valued experience, for I remain one of those wanderers who relish the stimulation of any journey – even (would you believe?) that airline food! Fresh from Treasure Island and his South Sea adventures, Robert Louis Stevenson seemed to me to get it about right, a century ago: "For my part, I travel not to go anywhere, but to go. I travel for travel's sake. The great affair is to move."

I have been carrying-on that Great Affair, in public, for years – and remain deeply devoted. After umpteen million miles following my wandering star, I still find myself excited at the thought of each new journey – even if it's merely down the road a piece; still devour the airline schedules and wonder whether I should be setting off towards some new experience. The prospect of a strange new scene always excites, and on the way towards it I always want the corner seat, to see what's happening...

So to me this book seems like frozen documentary – instant Whicker's World, if you like – for almost every page can unleash a powerful memory. Let's hope some of the glories lying in wait behind this foreword may also get *you* off and running, for in the troubled state of our world today the more we see of each other, the better.

So whether you move through space or through pages, a look round the world's riches does nothing but good; and remember, we travellers even receive wise encouragement from the Bible, in Daniel 12:24: "Many shall run to and fro, and knowledge shall be increased."

One of my closest friends says that if he could not have a camera with him, he would not bother to travel. Whilst this may be going a little further than some people, almost every photographer will have some sympathy for such an attitude. Apart, perhaps, from snapshots of loved ones, travel must be *the* most powerful stimulus to photography for most people.

Nevertheless, travel photography is a very wide field, and a little analysis of what we want from it can pay dividends. Broadly, there are four separate reasons for taking pictures when we travel. First, there is the personal souvenir; second, there is the desire to show other people; third, there are the commercial possibilities; and fourth, there is record photography on an expedition.

The first of these, the souvenir, is often despised by the 'serious' photographer; he calls it a mere snapshot. But what is wrong with snapshots? As long as you do not inflict them on other people, they are quite delightful and arguably give more pleasure than any other sort of photograph. They need not even be of a particularly high technical or artistic quality, though obviously you would usually prefer it if they were. The main purpose of the picture is to jog your memory, so the trick is to record whatever moves you: your memory will make up any shortcomings in the picture itself.

Inevitably, though, the people who most appreciate souvenirs are the people who were there. For a simple example, I could never understand why people treasured those wretched Alpine cowbells. Then I went to the Alps and heard them tinkling around the necks of the cows, and suddenly I understood. This brings us to our second reason.

If you want to show the pictures to other people, you have to be rather more selective and thoughtful. They were not there: unless they know the place well, they will not be able to smell the incense and dung fires, feel the thin night wind, or recall the stars sparkling in the sky. You have, perhaps, to be more obvious.

It is probably impossible, though, to shoot pictures *only* for other people. Often, the most successful pictures are the ones which you really shot for yourself. You were so stunned by a place, made to feel so alive by its beauty or strangeness or

majesty, that you were determined to capture at least a part of this on film. This is rather different from the snapshot, which is a much more lightweight kind of picture, because it is a more universal experience.

The third reason, commerce, is not one which we shall touch upon much in this book. This is because it is generally more concerned with being a businessman than with being a photographer; it is another layer grafted onto the ability to take pictures. A lot of this is mere administrative detail, such as arranging *carnets* for the import and export of equipment, marshalling models, and so forth, but there are some ways in which it also affects the photography.

For example, because most travel photography is used to illustrate articles or advertisements concerning holidays, it has to present a somewhat idealised picture of the world. Skies are always blue, the sun always shines, and everything is clean and sanitary. I particularly remember one picture I took of a very small Tibetan monk, about eight years old, with a very large bicycle. It is an amusing and charming picture; but there is a small pile of dung by the bicycle wheel, which is enough to put off the commercial picture buyer.

There are also compositional differences. Tightly-composed pictures are generally less popular than those which can be cropped in various ways by the picture editor to suit a layout, and large and relatively blank areas of foreground or blue sky, which would normally be regarded as fairly undesirable, suddenly become a selling point – they provide somewhere to put the text! If you are of the Henri Cartier-Bresson school, and refuse to allow anyone ever to crop your pictures, you would do well to stay out of commercial photography.

In addition, almost all commercial photography is done on rollfilm or even large-format cameras. This is not only because they provide higher-quality pictures; it is also a demonstrable fact that a picture editor going through a stack of pictures can see the bigger images more easily without recourse to a magnifier, and this makes them easier to sell.

Our fourth approach, namely expedition photography, itself falls into two sub-divisions. First, there are the pictures taken to illustrate the expedition, which have a lot in common with any other pictures taken to show other people. A more structured and rigorous approach is needed in order that a complete picture of the expedition's activities can be shown.

The second sub-division is less concerned with the attractiveness of the pictures than with the information they hold, which is to furnish either the raw data for further research or a straightforward technical record of what was done – as, for example, in archaeological photography. Although this is a specialised field, it is one which many a skilled photographer may become involved with, as well as one in which there are a number of specialised techniques which can be of considerable use in more general photography.

No matter what pictures you take or why, the golden rule is to remember that the criteria for successful pictures do not suddenly and magically change just because you are away from home. You will need to apply every bit as much effort and experience in your travel photography as you would at home, if you want first-class pictures. Against that, travel photography is inevitably different from staying at home, if only because of the novelty and excitement of it all.

I do not promise that by the time you have read this book you will know all there is to know about travel photography: I do not think that anyone knows that, let alone myself, and even if they did I doubt if it would be communicable. What I do promise is that if you read the text, study the pictures, and read the captions – all three are designed to work together, and none should stand alone – you will be saved a great deal of the trial and error which I and many other photographers have already been through.

WHERE?

Regardless of where you are going, there is a great deal to be said for finding out as much as you possibly can about the place before you actually leave. Quite apart from the fact that such anticipatory research is in itself enjoyable, it can make an enormous difference to the quality of the results you bring back.

First of all, do not neglect the sheer foreignness of where you are going. Few have ever died of culture shock, but it has been known to make an awful lot of people very unhappy. In India, for example, my wife found that the only way she could avoid leers and stares from men was to cover her head with a shawl and drop her eyes: the old American ideal of holding the head high and looking the world in the eye had to go by the board. Unless you are prepared to make this degree of adaptation, you may do well to forget travelling to the more remote parts of the world.

Secondly, find out about the practical details of where you will be going. What will the weather be like? Are you going to have to rely on some form of public transport once you are there? If so, what is it like? What will it cost? How reliable is it, and how comfortable? Remember that seasons can be very different in other countries – in India, again, the monsoon season is in what is to most Westerners the late summer; everything is permanently soaking wet, and most people are agreed that life is very unpleasant indeed. Even if the seasons are more or less the same, there can be other factors which can govern when you go to a place. I remember visiting a friend in Paris, many years ago, in August; it was like a ghost town, as everyone had taken their summer holidays simultaneously.

Thirdly, you should try to find out all you can about the sort of things which you want to photograph. For example, are you attracted by mountains, or by castles, or by beaches? Although to most people a travel photographer is primarily concerned with beaches, I have never found them particularly visually interesting; mountains, cities at night and people are what turn me on photographically. Remember, too, that there may be special attractions which are only on at certain times of the year – the famous Munich Oktoberfest is one example, and just to confuse you the majority of the Oktoberfest is in September!

Although research is in many ways the most enjoyable part of the planning, it does carry with it one severe danger: that of trying to fit in too much. It is very much better to concentrate on two or three things than to rush madly about trying to cover half a dozen. This is not nanny-type advice: I have tried it, and quite apart from the fact that it is exhausting it means that you miss out on many pictures which present themselves serendipitously, simply because you are too busy to notice them. It also means that instead of spending a day looking around and getting into the subject, you try to photograph everything first time. Whilst there is a good deal to be said for the freshness of vision which this engenders, it also means that you *know* that there are a lot of pictures which you miss because you do not have time to come back to them.

Finally, you should investigate any difficulties which might arise, and make preparations for them. They will fall into four groups, but unfortunately it is impossible to tell until after the trip which problem will fall into what group.

The only really agreeable problems are the ones which do not arise: for example, customs inspections can be anything from a nightmare to insignificant. They are usually the latter, but it is as well to be prepared for the worst.

The second group consists of what one might call potential problems – problems which will almost certainly arise unless you take the appropriate precautions, but which equally certainly will not arise if you do. Examples include getting visas, arranging foreign money and taking reasonable care of your possessions so that they are not stolen.

The third group consists of the minor hassles which are attendant upon almost any trip, but which are minimised if you know what to do. For example, in many countries a small bribe will work wonders; in others, it will land you in jail.

The last and most serious group is real trouble: getting thrown in the local slammer, bloody-minded customs and immigration officials, and so forth. The main thing to remember is that this sort of thing happens very rarely indeed, and that when it does happen it is as often as not the result of the visitor's own actions or attitude.

Often, you are likely to have transgressed without realising it, or to have committed some offence which seems minor to you but far from minor to the person who apprehended you. In the former case, a suitably apologetic stance may well get you out of it; in the latter, you have to emphasise that you appreciate that you were being foolish, to apologise sincerely, and (unusually) to offer to make what redress you can *without making it look like a bribe*. Given that you have probably had the misfortune to be nobbled by someone rather officious, a bribe is likely to make things look even worse.

Almost invariably, a combination of patience and sweet reason will get you out of trouble – though you may be rather shaken by the experience. Incidentally, do not imagine that obstructive bureaucracy is the prerogative of 'foreigners'. I am Cornish and my wife is American: we have both had our share of hassles with immigration control, especially before we were married. The U.S. authorities have a more rigid attitude, whilst the British win hands down on Kafkaesque slowness and inscrutability, with a fair number of Catch-22 situations thrown in. If things get really bad, all you can do is to demand to see a diplomatic representative of your own country, and hope they let you.

LEARNING ABOUT A COUNTRY

The big question is how you find out all that you need to know about a country, and the straight answer is that you cannot; unless you live there all your life, there will be occasions when suddenly something takes you by surprise. You can, however, soften the blow considerably.

You can begin with the tourist image of a country. Most countries maintain a tourist office in the capital of each of the major nations, and these can be a fruitful source of free information. Most give out excellent maps, too – the Germans are particularly good – as well as guides to accommodation and specific regional guides. If you want really detailed information, especially about a particular area, you can write to the appropriate Tourist Board in its own native land.

Although the information available from the tourist board is usually (and predictably) fairly heavily biased, it does give you a good starting point and also provides a fair amount of basic information, such as when national holidays are, what visas and inoculations (if any) are required, and perhaps best of all information about special events, fairs, festivals, and so forth.

Your next line of attack might be a travel agent, though I have generally found these to be acutely uninformed about what a place is actually like; they are much better when it comes to sorting out fares and accommodation which is, after all, what they are there for. Some also have useful tables of average temperatures, average hours of sunlight, and so on.

Next, there is the public library and the bookshop. What I usually do is to buy the books with hard information – the Michelin Guide, or the Guide Bleu, or the excellent Frommer books which started out as '$5 a day' and have been subject to steady inflation ever since – and read the background stuff (including picture books) from the library. Books like the Frommers' 'Dollarwise' guides can not only pay for themselves several times over; they can also save much effort and heartbreak hunting in the wrong places. Every now and then I meet people who consider such guides beneath their dignity: no 'real' traveller, they say, would use them. However, at the time of writing, I had travelled about 50,000 miles in the previous twelve months, by air, sea, train, car and motorcycle, plus a fair amount by bus. I find Frommerese gushing English a little too much for my aesthetic sensibilities, but otherwise I have absolutely no hesitation in saying that they are amongst the finest investments you can make – provided they cover the area you need!

After this, you may be lucky enough to meet people who have been where you are going, or to see films or attend lectures or talks. All of these can be invaluable, although, of course, the better you know the person in question the more you will be able to judge the value of what they are saying. I lived in Malta for four years when I was a child, and loved it; but even among my childhood friends there were people who hated it because it was not enough like England. It was, they complained, hot, dirty and smelly – which it was, but so what? If you are into insults, England is cold, rainy and miserable.

The last and most useful way of finding out about a place is to visit it, no matter how briefly. Once, when I was researching another book, I covered 2,500 miles in two weeks on a motorcycle – the classic 'seven countries in fourteen days'. I touched on a number of places I had never been before; and whilst I admit that so brief an acquaintance is scarcely a sound foundation for balanced judgement, a number of my preconceptions were considerably modified.

This also illustrates that no matter what anyone says, you should always treat it with reserve. Whilst it is true that there are some places on earth that are so beautiful as to be universally accepted as such – like the Himalayas, the Austrian Tyrol, and parts of California – there is also the matter of personal taste and experience. What one person loves, another may loathe; and where one person found a friendly welcome, superb food and beautiful weather, another may find surliness, slop and rain. I have lived in many places, and for each of them I can remember days which would put anyone off for life and others which would make an addict of anyone; it is all down to luck.

It may seem that so far I have talked a great deal about travel and not so much about photography, but this is inevitable; it would be a very one-dimensional book which did not consider where you were going and what you were doing before talking about how to photograph it. As with photographing anything else, you really have to care about what you are photographing before you can consistently photograph it well. I like people and landscapes, and so these are what I photograph, at home or abroad.

This returns us to the question I asked at the beginning of the book: why are you taking photographs? Whilst you are doing your preliminary research, you are more than likely to start thinking of pictures you want to take. As you do so, start asking yourself questions. How much has your chosen place or subject been photographed before? What scope is there for originality? This can be particularly important if you are taking pictures for more than just the family album or the domestic slide show. If the subject is very well known – the burning ghats at Benares, for example, or London's big, red buses – then your audience may well have a favourite image, or even a series of images, with which they will consciously or unconsciously be comparing your work.

At this point you have to make a choice. Are you going to omit the obvious shot, so that it does not invite comparison, or shoot it in some totally novel way so that it reveals new aspects of itself to the viewer, or are you going to try for a really superb version of one of the more clichéd views? One travel photographer of my acquaintance has an excellent line in showing more than you expect of a building – the Taj Mahal in its surroundings, for example, or the hollowness of the Palace of the Winds – whereas I tend to omit the absolutely standard landmarks (which are already more than adequately covered anyway) and concentrate on beauty, wherever I may find it. I never did like the Eiffel Tower, anyway. If I *have* to produce one of the picture-postcard shots, I set it up very carefully on a tripod and shoot it on 6x7cm format so that what it lacks in originality it at least recovers in quality. Remember that in some sorts of photography the obvious pictures – what the movie-makers call 'establishing shots' – are essential; some sponsors will expect them, and in any case they can literally be used to establish a location.

The second half of this book deals at considerable length with the subjects in front of your camera, but the first deals with all the things which you have to attend to before you go. Whilst on one level this might be seen as tedious, on another it prolongs your holiday so that it lasts for several months before you go; there is nothing like getting your equipment together, checking it out, and researching the place you are intending to visit to make the trip come alive for you.

Always, though, there is one thing to remember: it is impossible to take travel pictures in isolation. There is an old saying that it is better to travel hopefully than to arrive; what we want is to do both. Bon voyage!

TRAVEL AT HOME

The idea of 'travel at home' seems a strange one, but it is actually quite a useful exercise. What you do is to pretend that you are visiting your home town, or the countryside in which you live, and plan your photography as already outlined. If you want to make it slightly more interesting, you can choose somewhere a little further away, but still well within the compass of a day trip or at most a weekend.

First of all, sort out the salient points of your city. As an example, I will take a city I know well and in which I spent many years: Plymouth.

First and foremost, Plymouth is a naval port. This automatically brings to mind the port, the Royal Naval Dockyard, and the civil docks, as well as the few fishing boats which still work from them.

Historically, it is probably most famous for two things: Sir Francis Drake's voyages and his repulse of the Spanish Armada, and the sailing of the *Mayflower*. Obviously, both these things are commemorated, and it might be worthwhile taking pictures of the memorials. Sir Francis Drake's house, Buckland Abbey, is a fair way outside Plymouth: a side-trip would not be practical unless you are spending a few days down there.

During the Second World War, Plymouth was mercilessly bombed. There are a few medieval and Elizabethan buildings remaining, but the whole of the centre was redeveloped after the war with a relatively undistinguished style of architecture laid out on a fairly rigorous block system. The Civic Centre is a very high building, and there is a public viewing platform on top which is (usually) open; this gives the chance of some interesting 'aerial' shots.

The Hoe, of course, is famous, and a surprising amount of open space still exists; a lot of parades, both civil and military, take place on it. There is also on the Hoe a lighthouse, Smeaton's Tower, which was disassembled from the Eddystone Rock when the new lighthouse was built; it is open to the public, and it offers a rare chance to see the inside of a real built-for-work, isolated lighthouse.

That little lot would provide more than enough for a day's photography, and I have not yet mentioned the mock-Gothic Plymouth College; the soaring suspension bridge over the Tamar; the Egyptian-influenced architecture from the early eighteenth century in Devonport; the chain-driven ferry at Torpoint; Royal William Yard, the old navy victualling yard, a beautiful piece of Georgian architecture; Central Park; or the cobbles of the Barbican.

Near at hand, there is the ancient Stannary town of Tavistock, with its Friday market (and Plymouth's own market should not be neglected); Sir Francis Drake's house, as already mentioned; numerous villages such as Buckland Monachorum and Milton Combe, or Meavy, with ancient pubs and churches; Sheepstor church, where the White Rajahs of Sarawak are buried, and, of course, Dartmoor itself.

From such an exercise, you can also learn how easy it is to try to fit in too much. Widecombe-in-the-Moor, known to many only through the song *Widecome Fair*, actually exists. The temptation to go to it might seem considerable if you are only looking at the map, but in real life it is a long drive through country lanes – at least half a day gone.

You can derive still more benefit if you actually go out and try to photograph all these things. Of course, you can miss out the ones which do not interest you, but you should still find plenty to do. This may be a useful shot in the arm for your regular photography, and if you treat it as a genuine travel-type exercise, not allowing yourself to nip home and fetch something you had forgotten, you will learn a great deal. Take note of what you actually *use*, as distinct from what you take with you – that can be every bit as valuable!

This sort of exercise can, with advantage, be repeated for each of the kinds of subject described in the book. You will be freed of the difficulty of working in a foreign land with a foreign language, and all the hassles of customs, passports, immigration, and so forth will be irrelevant. Try gaining access to factories, for example: in Plymouth, the Plymouth Gin distillery might be a good starting point. Once you have done it in English, you are likely to find it very much easier to get into a brewery in Munich, Solan, or Amsterdam – and you will have a better idea of what to photograph.

The selection of equipment must, of course, be a major part of planning an expedition or trip of any kind, and that is what we shall look at next; but remember, if you try it out under typical working conditions at home, you will be all the better able to use it when you travel.

EQUIPMENT

'How long is a piece of string?' runs the old schoolboy riddle. 'Half an inch shorter than you need' comes the cynical reply. So much depends on where you are going, what you want to do, and what sort of results you want that it is impossible to recommend any one outfit. The important thing is not what you have got: it is whether what you have got can do the job.

Consequently, I have divided equipment notes into three sections. The first is a minimalist approach, the second is what one might call 'serious' photography – to professional or semi-professional standards – and the third deals with what happens when you go 'off the beaten track'.

THE BARE BONES

To a large extent, the minimum you can bear to take with you depends very much on the kind of photographer you are. If you are having difficulties in deciding what you will need, I suggest the following: one camera and two lenses.

There are a number of advantages in paring your equipment to the bone. The first is that it is easy to carry; you are not grunting under half a hundredweight of gear. The second is that security is much less of a problem. If you are carrying a small fortune in camera equipment, it is hard not to get paranoid about theft; if you do not have much, it is easier to carry with you and in any case you do not stand to lose so much if it is stolen. The third is more subtle: if you are not obsessed with photographing everything you see, you can devote more time to just enjoying yourself. Just because you enjoy photography does not mean that you have to be its slave!

The obvious choice is 35mm equipment, though the very minimum – a compact camera with a fixed lens of around 35 or 40mm – is probably a bit too minimal for most people. It is possible to survive with a single lens, but it usually has to be something reasonably exotic: I would plump for a 35mm f/1.4, whilst my wife favours her 35-85mm f/2.8 Vivitar Series 1 zoom. Otherwise, two lenses give you very much more choice. The focal lengths and apertures will depend on your personal tastes (and the state of your bank balance!), but for most people it is not hard to decide which lens is used for 90% of your photography, and which other one accounts for the next 9%. The figures may be a slight exaggeration, but it is surprising just how much you do use one or two lenses. I have always been an addict of wide-angles, so a 24mm and a 50mm – the latter as fast as possible – would be my choice. I know someone else who normally packs a 70-210mm zoom and a 500mm f/8 mirror lens, on the other hand.

If you really cannot stand the worry of working with a single body, then take another one along – but treat it strictly as a spare, and leave it in the hotel safe (or hide it under your dirty washing) unless the other one breaks down.

A serious alternative, though a rather unfashionable one nowadays, is to pack an old twin-lens reflex such as a Rolleiflex. You could even pack a new Yashica TLR; the Mamiya Interchangeable-lens model, versatile though it is, introduces too much complexity for our minimal approach. Most TLRs are virtually indestructible, provide superb image quality on a big piece of film and, with the addition of a couple of close-up lenses, can tackle just about anything. Usually, you will need a separate light-meter, but this is no great problem. The image quality, together with the ruggedness, makes this an option well worth considering if you *have* to bring back high-quality pictures, whether to satisfy a sponsor or for publication or exhibition.

SERIOUS PHOTOGRAPHY

There must be a fundamental division here between 'grab' shots and those which are more carefully considered. For the one, 35mm will be almost everyone's choice: for the other, the choice of camera type is more open and the basis for choice is quite different.

I do quite a lot of 'grab' shooting myself, and I use the same equipment as many photographers far greater than I: an old Leica. In fact, I use two, an M2 and an M3, with just three lenses: 35mm f/1.4, 50mm f/1.2, and 85mm f/2. The sheer speed of the lenses – especially the 35/1.4 – is often invaluable when the light is poor or at night, and the speed and ease of focusing of the rangefinder Leica has to be experienced to be believed.

Whilst these are widely regarded as the ultimate, they are certainly not the only possible choice. I used to use Nikons with a range of lenses from 21mm to 200mm, all as fast as I could afford (even the 200mm was an f/3!), but I decided that the Leicas were quicker in use. The important thing is to remember that no matter what you use, you must know your way around it almost instinctively. You must be able to focus without even thinking about it, and to change shutter speed or aperture by a stop or more in either direction without

looking: the time you waste checking settings can make the difference between success and failure.

You must also keep your equipment to a minimum, as time spent changing lenses is often wasted: you can usually get the effect you want faster and more easily by walking a few paces closer to your subject or moving a few paces further away. I find that a 35mm or 50mm lens on a 35mm camera is usually all that I need, and when I am in my photojournalist mode I tend to carry the two Leicas together, one above the other. The chrome M2 with the 35mm lens is on the shorter strap, and the black M3 with the 50mm lens is below it; a meter lives on the M2, for checking exposure. Both bodies are loaded with the same speed film, so that I do not have to waste time sorting that out. The fact that one is chrome and the other black is not just ostentation (though I have to admit that it suits the image very well): it makes grabbing the right one just that much easier, and if I am using both colour and black and white (which is desirable sometimes) I keep the black-and-white in the chrome body and the colour in the black one. Most people do it the other way around, so do whatever suits you.

When sheer speed of action is not required, though, there is a lot to be said for the reflex camera. Most people find it much easier to compose a picture on the clearly-defined ground-glass screen than in the brightlines of a viewfinder, and a much wider range of lenses is both available and practicable. Despite the indisputable fact that wide-angles for reflexes are harder to design than wide-angles for non-reflex cameras, unless you want extreme speed the difference in quality is not very high, and perspective is much easier to judge. With long lenses, reflex focusing is all but essential anyway: coupling anything longer than 135mm to a rangefinder is risky, and getting a viewfinder which points in the right direction is even more problematical.

This brings us to the more carefully considered shots, and I make an immediate and impassioned plea for the tripod. Regardless of the sort of camera you are using, if you put it on a tripod you stand to gain immensely. First, the picture will be sharper and clearer; second, you are likely to compose the picture much more carefully; and third, the discipline of setting up the tripod will make you less hurried, and more inclined to wait until the shot is right. I remember stopping in the Alps once, and saying 'What I need on this road is a red Mercedes in the foreground'. I had to wait about three or four minutes after setting the camera up...Austrians seem to like red Mercedes cars.

Many people have trouble in choosing the perfect camera case. I am no exception, but I have every bit as much trouble in choosing the perfect tripod. At the time of writing, I owned four: a dinky Leitz table-top model, about 6" high but doubling as a shoulder-pod; a Benbo, probably the most versatile and ingenious tripod ever made; a Gitzo Reporter, which folds up very compactly and will (just!) fit inside the Krauser panniers on my BMW; and a Sachtler Hollywood, with a custom-made levelling bowl/ball and socket head, which is ridiculously light and exquisitely made. Actually, there is a fifth – but as it weighs 28lb and is used only with my big field cameras, I feel justified in excluding it.

It is a fundamental amateur failing that all else is subordinated to the camera: in order to possess a Nikon, say, or a Canon, economies are made elsewhere which make a mockery of the potential of the camera. Most amateur tripods are a rather wobbly joke, which is reflected in their price and weight. A good tripod (excepting table-top models) is very unlikely to weigh less than 6lb complete with head and will cost as much as a good compact camera or a cheap SLR: there is no real way around this, short of buying second-hand (which is not a bad idea, as faults in any tripod are easily spotted, and in a second-hand one they become downright obvious). The Sachtler is an exception to the weight limit, but you pay for it.

If you decide to use 35mm – and there is little reason not to, unless you want to sell your pictures or are simply captivated by the image quality of bigger formats – your equipment will be reasonably light and easy to carry, but you must guard against the tendency to carry everything including the kitchen sink simply because you have it. A good approach is to select a modest-sized camera bag, a subject we shall return to later, and fill that with the gear that you will need.

Once again, this will depend very much on the sort of pictures you plan on taking, but try to analyse what they are and you may well find that equipment selection becomes easier. As a basic outfit, consider four lenses: one wide-angle of around 24mm or 28mm, the standard lens, a modest zoom of around 80-200mm, and one other lens; something very long, perhaps, or something fast, or even a specialised lens such as a shift lens for architectural photography.

If you do not like zooms, then you will probably have to substitute with two other lenses: I like a 90mm or 105mm and a 200mm, with the added advantage that my 90mm is a macro lens and will go down to 1:2 without its adaptor and 1:1 with it. An additional advantage to this approach is that the two fixed-length lenses are very much faster than the zoom: a 90mm f/2.5 and a 200mm f/3 represent at least a stop over any zoom unless you go mad and spend a fortune – and fast zooms are so big and heavy that you might as well carry two fixed lenses anyway.

Add in a teleconverter. No-one actually *likes* these things, as they do cause a noticeable deterioration in image quality and they also lose speed. I find that a 1.4x is not really worth the effort; I prefer to lose another stop and go to 2x, but 3x is altogether too much. The big advantage of teleconverters is that they are very compact, they are not very expensive, and if you need 400mm when the longest lens you have is a 200mm, they get you out of trouble. Many professionals use them – but only when they have to.

Two bodies is a reasonable complement, both as insurance against mechanical failure and for convenience's sake; if you carry both, you can load them with different emulsions or use them with two different lenses – maybe one on the tripod and one hand-held. Three bodies is verging on paranoia.

A lens hood is all but essential: sure, you can take pictures without it, but they will lack saturation and may well show flare patterns. For still better saturation, use a polarising filter *as well* – the difference it makes, by cutting out reflected white light, has to be seen to be believed. The only other filters you will normally need are clear or UV filters, for mechanical protection of the lens (most modern lenses are so 'warm' in colour rendition that there is no need to filter out the UV, even in the mountains) and an 81A or stronger warming filter which makes sunny scenes just a little bit sunnier and grey ones a little less grey. You may wish to consider daylight-to-artificial-light filters if you plan on shooting much at night; the subject is covered at greater length when we look at films.

A valuable accessory for sunny climes is a small flashgun to use for fill-in flash; it is virtually essential if you want to try any glamour-type shots, as otherwise it is very difficult indeed to expose for both the subject and the surroundings. You may also wish to consider a much bigger flashgun for general use, and a useful option is to have two or three small guns with built-in slave units if you want to try anything clever on location.

There are a number of other minor accessories and doodads, some of which may not seem obviously photographic at first but most of which will prove very useful very quickly. Briefly, they are:

A cable release (or two, as they are easy to lose).

Blower brush and lens tissues (remember that 'tinned wind' explodes if it gets too hot – use it in the studio, not on location).

Small screwdrivers (vibration when travelling can loosen small screws).

A hand-held meter such as a Weston or Lunasix.

Lens caps, front and rear, for all lenses.

A really versatile pocket knife.

A little gaffer tape; some string and/or thread (try linen button thread – incredibly strong); some paper clips (a useful source of wire); a few elastic bands; some cyanoacrylate adhesive, such as Superglue.

A spirit level for setting the camera true on the tripod.

The knife goes in your pocket, and the rest takes up very little room in your camera bag.

Speaking of camera bags, there must be a fortune awaiting the man who designs the perfect one. There is no one camera bag which can do everything: they are all compromises. For shipping and travelling, aluminium-skinned cases such as Halliburton and Rox are the very best, but they do have their drawbacks. One is that they practically have STEAL ME written all over them, as they are so recognisably camera bags; another is that they are big and heavy, and have to be laid on a flat surface for use; and the third is that the snug-fitting foam rubber linings are a bit too snug for fast use in the field. Furthermore, they are hard to move when they are open, so you may wander further from your bag than is wise.

A good alternative, though it does not offer quite the same protection, is the compartmented fitted case. Hasselblad make some lovely ones, and the little leather Bach'o cases hold a remarkable amount (I can get in two bodies, five lenses, and a lot of accessories, plus some film). They are smaller and lighter (though very heavy when filled) and a bit quicker to use than the foam-filled variety – the Fiberbilt case, with its padded partitions which can be rearranged in so many ways, is especially handy.

For field use, most people prefer soft bags. There are huge numbers of these, with the very best probably coming from Lowe. Billingham bags are attractive and well made, but do not offer very much protection. Whatever you do, do *not* just throw your cameras and lenses into the bag unprotected. It is not just the cosmetic appearance which will suffer: chips, dust, and stiff focusing movements will all bear mute witness to abuse.

An alternative to the soft bag is the photographer's waistcoat or jerkin (or vest as it is called in the United States). These are wonderful things; you can carry a vast amount of gear with great security and without getting tired, and it is always accessible. The only problems come when you want to go through doors, or sit down and have a drink, when you begin to feel like the Michelin man.

There are also various belts and bandoliers, which do not carry much but can save the day when all you have to carry is a couple of extra lenses and some film, with perhaps a meter. I actually use all of the above, and I am still looking; one of my more interesting camera boxes is a solid-leather affair bought from a government surplus store, with EXPLODER DYNAMO CONDENSER MK II on the lid; it has got me into trouble more than once...

One thing which has hardly been mentioned at all so far is medium and large format equipment. This is partly because it is comparatively little used by amateurs, and partly because you have to be fairly dedicated to carry it on holiday with you. Having said that, I would be the last person to knock it. Even if I were not trying to sell my pictures, I think that I would still use medium format because of the beautiful quality which is possible. The actual weight to be carried is usually not that much greater than 35mm, largely because you tend to take so much less gear with you: three lenses is normally the limit for most people, and the availability of interchangeable backs means that there is no great need to carry two bodies.

Nor is the running cost that much higher, because although the per-exposure cost is about four times as much, you tend to be a lot more careful about each picture – 'machine-gun' tactics lose their appeal. The more considered approach also means that the pictures are often better – I know that as a general rule (though one often broken) the longer I take thinking about a shot and setting it up, the better it will be.

With the right medium-format camera you also get several other advantages. Many take Polaroid backs, which are invaluable not just for checking pictures but also for checking the camera and for taking pictures of people to give as presents. A few – such as my own Linhof – also give you camera movements, which are indispensable for serious architectural photography.

The choice of medium-format cameras is considerable, with most of the different marques having their own particular selling points. I used to use Linhof and Hasselblad, but now I use Linhof and Mamiya, for several reasons. One is the sheer cost of a Hasselblad and its accessories, but another is the difficulty of focusing close with a Hassel. You need expensive close-up lenses, which are far less convenient than the RB67's continuous bellows action. I also like the larger format of the RB67; by the time you have cropped the square format to a usable rectangle, the effective area of the 6x7cm format is 50-75% bigger, rather than the 20% or so that simple comparison of the areas might suggest.

Of course, the RB67 has its drawbacks. It is considerably bigger and heavier than the Hasselblad, and at f/3.8 the standard lens is close to a stop slower; but I have an f/2.8 Planar on the Linhof, so I do not miss that.

I am also fortunate in that I work as a team with my wife, who is a photographer in her own right, and she uses Mamiya 645 equipment. The 'baby' Mamiya – she uses the 1000S – can be fitted with an f/1.9 standard lens of quite high quality, which allows roll-film quality with a whole stop's advantage over the opposition. The 15-on format is effectively little smaller than 12-on, because of the cropping already mentioned, and it provides a useful 50% increase over the 10-on 6x7cm format in film economy. The only thing I have against the 645 is that it is totally battery dependent – we *always* carry a tested spare, and usually a mechanical back-up camera as well (though we have never had to use it yet).

It should not be thought, though, that 12-on is dead. In fact, many art directors prefer a square picture, as they can crop it vertically or horizontally to suit their layout. This is primarily a commercial advantage, though, and I for one have my doubts about it. After all, I try not to compose my shots so loosely that they could be used either portrait or landscape, and I suspect that any shot so composed might lose out when compared with a properly-composed rectangular picture.

Large format cameras, by which I mean those taking cut film, are another matter. Although they deliver superb quality, and are still used by a few specialist travel photographers for that reason, for most people they are just a bit too much trouble, mostly because of the difficulties of film loading and unloading on location. Even if you have four Grafmatic backs, each of which holds six sheets of film, you will still have to reload after twenty-four exposures – which is not much for a whole trip, especially if you are shooting two exposures of each subject, one to hold and one to process. Sorting out the 'process' and 'hold' films, and retrieving the 'hold' ones if the first ones prove to be a little over or under exposed, is also pretty wearing. It is worth remembering, though, that at night with the room light off the windowless bathroom found in so many hotels is an excellent darkroom. Alternatively, you could use a changing bag.

OFF THE BEATEN TRACK

Going away from areas in which you can take normal Western comforts for granted makes quite a number of changes to the way you look at your equipment. First and foremost, you must carry everything with you – you will not be able to buy film (even at ruinous prices) if you run out in the Himalayas, and you can forget about spare batteries.

Secondly, you will need very reliable equipment which will not break down and leave you unable to get the pictures of a lifetime. This means that simplicity counts for a lot, and that you should never be without a backup. There are certain cameras which have tremendous reputations for indestructibility, and it is well worth considering one of these: Leica, Nikon F, Rolleiflex, Linhof.

Thirdly, you will probably physically have to carry your

equipment from time to time, possibly for quite long distances, so the weight must be kept down. You may need to 'harden' your carrying equipment, too: I remember one journey from Dehra Dun to Delhi, in alternate dust and rain, when one of my Halliburtons had to ride on the roof of an Indian bus.

With all this in mind, it pays you to consider very carefully what you are going to take. First of all, go through all your equipment and check out *everything* which requires a battery. The standard advice is to replace all batteries, but this can get a bit extravagant: unless they have been in use for a good few months already, simply carrying spares – for *everything* – will be enough. Test the spares with a meter, or have the shop do it for you: it is by no means unknown for 'fresh' batteries to be all but dead.

Try, as far as possible, to use non-battery-dependent equipment, or at least to have it for a back-up. Remember that hot and humid climates can wreak havoc with electrical contacts, and that very cold ones can dramatically reduce the effective power of batteries. A Weston Master is an excellent idea; they are superbly accurate in their own right, very reliable, and completely independent of batteries. Remember that if you use mechanical equipment, it may be within the skill of the local watchmaker or someone similar to effect a repair – it is normally only a matter of cleaning out some dirt – but electronics require sophisticated test equipment and replacement modules.

If you are using fairly old equipment, or equipment you have bought second-hand, you may consider it worthwhile investing in a strip-clean-and-overhaul; if this is done by someone really good, it can be money very well spent. The old advice about never going abroad with an untried, new camera applies equally to an untried, repaired camera!

Alternatively, have a 'check-up'. Many manufacturers or their agents will do this for a nominal fee, and even if you have to pay a repairer it will not cost much. If you are going somewhere really bitterly cold, consider having the camera 'winterised' – all the lubricants cleaned out and replaced with much thinner oils. This is nothing like as necessary as it used to be, and is really only recommended for cameras which are going to be used for long periods – several months – in bad weather. Usually, you can get by by keeping the camera under your coat until you want to use it.

Take very good care of your equipment in the field. Tape over any cracks where dust, rain, snow, etc. might penetrate. It is all very well to adopt the macho attitude that the camera can look after itself, but quite apart from the possible repair bill, you are going to look pretty silly if it stops working. Clean it each evening if necessary, and check out the various mechanical functions: shutter, diaphragm stopdown (easy to miss), and film transport.

On the other hand, remember that taking pictures is what you (and the camera!) are there for: you will accomplish nothing if you are permanently frightened to take the camera out of the bag.

There are all kinds of little hints and tips on looking after your equipment in harsh climates. For a start, a light-coloured camera bag will heat up (and cool down) much more slowly than a dark or black one: a black bag can 'cook' the film and even damage the camera if it is left out in the hot sun for a few hours. Plenty of padding not only protects from mechanical shock: it also helps with thermal shock, which occurs (for instance) when you go from an Alaskan winter into a centrally-heated house. To keep the dust out of a case, either use gaffer tape around the seams (this also provides excellent waterproofing) or make up a slip-cover with the seams as far as possible from the join on the case. Lightweight nylon is excellent, and you can seal the seams with iron-on tape.

In very humid climates, watch out for fungi and small beasties which want to eat the leather of the camera case and strap, the cotton or silk of the blind, and even the film itself. Use sealed cans and plenty of silica gel – it can be regenerated by heating on an iron plate in an oven. Beware of desiccating your equipment completely, though this is unlikely if you are only putting it away at night. In hot climates generally, dust is an insidious enemy: use lens caps front and back, and body caps when appropriate, all the time. Carry a piece of cotton or nylon if you want a working surface for changing lenses, etc. – at least it will avoid picking up anything but windblown dust.

Remember that the interior of a car, or the boot, can reach quite extraordinary temperatures in direct sunlight. And in cold weather, try to keep the camera as warm as possible (within reason!) as almost all shutters will slow down when they get cold. The temperatures at which this happens can range from a few degrees above freezing point to several degrees below. Leaf shutters will vary according to the type and condition of the lubricant – in most cases there should be so little that it is not noticeable – but focal-plane shutters can stiffen in their own right if they are of fabric instead of metal, quite apart from oils congealing.

All controls should be workable when wearing gloves, though loading will usually necessitate their removal. A transparent plastic bag keeps rain and snow out during reloading, and allows you to see what you are doing. In very cold weather, when humidity is very low (this can also apply in the desert), wind on slowly in order to avoid 'lightning flashes' due to static. Also, be aware that film can become brittle; fast winding can tear it. The same cautions apply in rewinding.

There is not much you can do about condensation, except

perhaps to leave the camera somewhere cold or to put it into the case and seal the case before you go indoors. Condensation is not a problem the first time you go out; it rears its ugly head when you come back in. What I normally do is to leave the camera somewhere reasonably cool, and when it has warmed up a bit put it in one of the warmer parts of the room to dispel the condensation. If you do get it, use a lens tissue to wipe it off the filter protecting the lens; it rarely affects the inside (rear) element, except in bellows cameras.

FILM, EXPOSURE, AND PROCESSING

When it comes to the selection of film, once again we return to the question of what the pictures are for. To most people, one of the chief creative stimuli in travel photography is the new colours; unless there is a very good reason for using black and white, or unless you are passionately devoted to the stuff, colour would seem to be the natural choice.

The two mains reasons why I would use black and white instead of colour are a desire to capture an Ansel Adams-type picture, with subtle and lovely gradations of black and white, or a yen for reportage work in poor light, perhaps with mixed tungsten and fluorescent lighting, rapidly changing and hard to meter. In the former case, the black and white image is a thing of beauty in itself, and in the latter there is the 'newsy' attraction of the immediacy and the fact that it is next to impossible to get a picture which has a respectable colour balance – though, as we shall see later, the strange colours which result from using colour films in difficult circumstances are seldom totally undesirable and are often an integral and important part of the picture.

In 35mm, the very different nature of these two approaches calls for two very different films: in the first case, Pan-F or Panatomic X, exposed with great care (and preferably bracketed) and processed in an extra-fine-grain developer such as Perceptol, and in the second, HP5 or Tri-X exposed at anything up to 1,600 ASA and processed in Microphen or another 'speed-increasing' developer. The equipment, of course, varies too: slow lenses and a tripod for the first, and the fastest lenses you have, used at full bore, for the second.

With rollfilm equipment, you can get away with medium-speed films for the Ansel Adams-type pictures, but given the generally slower lenses of rollfilm cameras the second type will call for very fast film indeed: HP5 or Tri-X again, or even 1,250 ASA Royal-X pan, which can be 'pushed' to 2,000 ASA with little loss of shadow detail. An elementary calculation shows that 2,000 ASA at f/2.8 is equivalent to 500 ASA at f/1.4; if you have the 110/2 Planar for the Hasselblad or the 80/1.9 for the Mamiya 645, this puts you a stop ahead of the game.

It is also possible with rollfilm equipment to use only XP-1 or another chromogenic black and white film but, despite the claims of many, I find it hard to believe that it can really equal both a fast and a slow conventional film simultaneously. For less extreme demands, it is wonderful; but not, I think, for this application.

Moving on to colour film, there is no doubt that for 'happy snaps' colour print films are unparalleled. Unless you are likely to want anything bigger than the usual wallet or postcard-sized prints, it is well worth considering standardising on 400 ASA: it is a little more expensive than the slower types, but its versatility is wonderful. If you are likely to be taking many pictures in poor light, it is even worth giving 1,000 ASA film a thought, as it will enable you to take some truly remarkable pictures.

If you want serious colour prints, on the other hand, the 100 ASA materials deliver perceptibly better results at 5x7" and significantly better ones at 10x8". As already mentioned, there are two main occasions when you might want to do this: first, when you want display prints for your own purposes, for home decoration or for an exhibition, and secondly when someone else – an expedition sponsor, say – specifically requests prints.

Otherwise, colour slides are the standard medium. In 35mm, almost all serious photographers who do not dislike its colour rendition use Kodachrome – and by this reference to its colour rendition I do not mean to imply that it is in any way inferior, simply that different films approximate reality in different ways, and that some people are more drawn to some films than to others.

The enormous advantages of Kodachrome are its superb grain and resolution, its impressive indifference to mistreatment (especially in the form of overheating), and its relatively low price. The first two are both consequences of its construction, which is unlike almost every other slide film ever made. Instead of incorporating the colour couplers in the emulsion, where they both make the emulsion thicker and are inclined to 'wander' under the influence of heat, they are added during processing. This means that the processing sequence is long, complex, and expensive, but it also keeps the cost of the filmstock down and, because it is virtually a black and white film until it is processed, makes Kodachrome almost indestructible by colour film standards.

Unfortunately, this superb film is not available in larger sizes, so the rollfilm user must content himself with other materials. The standard 64 ASA Ektachrome, called ER, is one of the most popular: others are Agfa's R100S, with a useful half-stop increase in speed, the various Agfa emulsions which are not compatible with E6 processing, and assorted Japanese offerings. One thing which you should avoid like the plague is the so-called 'professional' version of

any film: this is designed to be used in the studio, and processed almost immediately. If you let it get warm, or delay processing for too long, the results are likely to be quite significantly worse than with the regular variety.

Although some people swear by 25 ASA Kodachrome, there really is very little difference between the 25 ASA and the 64 ASA, and almost all professionals use the latter. The days when Kodachrome 25 was king, and Kodachrome 64 (or Kodachrome-X as it was then) was horrific are sufficiently fresh in the memory of many that the faster material still has a bad name: but for many years now it has been totally undeserved.

If you do need extra speed, the usual professional solution is to use 200 ASA Ektachrome (ED) and, where necessary, to push-process one stop; it is generally agreed that this still gives better results than using 400 ASA material, and it is a little bit cheaper, too. The 400 ASA really comes into its own in very mixed lighting, with fluorescents and neons and everything else, when it delivers surprisingly acceptable colours. Alternatively, 3M's 650 ASA artificial-light film also gives excellent results in such lighting, and can even be pushed one stop to 1,300 ASA. It is surprising, though, how often 400 ASA or 650 ASA is all that you need: it is much better to rely on ultra-fast lenses or longer exposures (with a tripod) than on push processing, unless you want greenish blacks and grain like golf balls.

The question of whether to use artificial-light films is not as easy to answer as it might seem. There is an old saying that 'colour can be as far out as you like, so long as it is warm', and this is surprisingly true in night photography – where, in any case, the colours are likely to be all over the place as a result of mixed light sources.

On the other hand, the extra speed of the 650 ASA 3M material can be very useful, especially when the alternatives are considered. You can use 400 ASA daylight type film, and risk (or accept) colour variations; you can use 160 ASA artificial-light film, and lose two stops in speed but gain a little in image quality; or you can use daylight-to-artificial-light conversion filters, but remember to focus before fitting the filter. The time a colour conversion filter is really useful is when trying to get something acceptable when the subject is lit with non-colour-corrected fluorescents: then, a CC20M or CC30M can give half-way tolerable results, though nothing can be done to get a *good* picture. The best results are normally to be had on 400 ASA film, I have found.

Apart from the regular 35mm slide films, there is now the option of the new Polaroid 35mm instant-transparency film. Whilst this is not very fast and, whilst the reseau pattern is fairly clearly visible even at modest magnifications, it does have its uses. It is invaluable, for instance, for checking that your camera is functioning properly, especially after a knock or use in adverse conditions, and the little images can also make useful presents, just as Polaroid prints from a larger camera can do.

You may also wish to use the venerable Agfa Dia-Direct black-and-white transparency film, or one of its new rapid-access Polaroid equivalents and, of course, the weird and interesting effects obtainable with infra-red 'false colour' films are well known. Unless you are already familiar with these, experiment with them before the trip – better to learn with unimportant images than with irreplaceable ones.

This applies equally to any other film: you should no more set out with an unknown film than with an unknown camera. It is by no means unusual to have to adjust the ASA rating slightly to suit personal preference, and it is better to find out what rating to use before you leave rather than after you come back. I have always found that with leaf shutters I am very close to the manufacturer's ASA rating, whereas with focal-plane shutters I often have to downrate the film by a third of a stop or so, so that 64 ASA becomes 50 and 200 ASA becomes 160. It must be some personal foible, but it has been true for years.

Metering in novel situations can be awkward, too. Often, people simply refuse to believe their meters and suffer as a result. The important thing is to be careful *what* you meter.

This is because all meters are designed on the assumption that all subjects reflect 18% of the light falling on them. This is surprisingly often true, but if (for example) you meter a white wall using an in-camera or other reflected-light meter, it is obviously not the case. The meter will still give a reading which will produce a *picture* that is an 18% grey, though, so the white wall comes out dark. If you want to keep it white, you must *increase* the exposure by anything up to three stops – though one or two will normally be enough. The same is true, of course, of snow. With dark subjects, the reverse is true, and you have to give a stop or two *less* exposure.

A much easier approach is to use an incident light meter, such as the Weston Master with an Invercone. The Invercone reflects 82% of the light falling on it, so that the meter reads its intended 18%.

You will still need to make some adjustments for very light and very dark subjects, but as a general rule all you need is half a stop *less* for bright subjects and half a stop *more* for dark ones; if in doubt, bracket an extra half stop in the direction already chosen.

Metering at night is very much a question of guesswork, but fortunately we can accept quite a wide range of exposures as 'correct', from those which just show a little highlight detail to those in which the background is as bright as day and parts are burned out. As a starting point, aim your in-camera or reflected-light meter at a light source more than a few feet away and give two or three stops more exposure than this indicates.

The question of bracketing is a vexed one. Many amateurs are acutely aware of the cost of film, and expect to get a good picture every time they press the button. A few professionals appear to care nothing for the price of film, and will shoot roll after roll of the same subject, at all possible apertures and most possible shutter speeds. A more realistic attitude than either lies somewhere in the middle.

Look at it this way: the trip is costing you plenty, and even if you tripled the amount you spent on film it would still be a pretty small part of the overall expenditure. If you shoot three shots of each subject – one as indicated, one a full stop over and one a full stop under – then tripling your film cost is exactly what you will do. What I do is to make plenty of exposures of something which I really care about, and want to get right, but take only a single shot if the subject is a snapshot or reference picture. I get through a lot of film, but I also get better results than if I counted the cost too carefully. Remember, too, that differences in exposure can make quite significant differences to the feel of a picture – one will not necessarily be better than another, just different. Bracketing keeps your options open.

Before we leave the subject of film, a brief note on processing. With black and white, doing it yourself is about the only way to get top-flight results without resorting to a very good and very expensive custom printer. This applies both to film processing and to printing. With colour print, a much better option is to have the film processed and proofed by a custom lab, and then either to print the ones you want yourself or to have a professional do it. Processing your own film is a snare and a delusion, as solution monitoring and quality control is likely to be far better in a custom lab than at home; it is usually cheaper, and often quicker unless you live too far from a lab.

For colour transparency processing, the only possible reason for doing it yourself is that you live too far from a decent lab to make it practical to have them do it. Use a professional lab – check out what the local professional photographers use – and let them take the strain. The control of colour processing is extremely complicated, and if they are doing it full time they are much more likely to get it right than you are if you only do it for a few hours a month. Their chemicals will be fresher and better monitored, their temperature control accurate as a matter of course, and their timing accurate. Sure, they may make the occasional mistake from time to time – but you will make more. Amateur labs are usually a lot less careful, and may scratch or fingerprint film, use solutions for too long, and generally take less care. There are a few really good amateur labs, but if you buy on price alone you will generally get what you pay for.

BUREAUCRACY

Hassles with officialdom are seldom the subject of a chapter in a photographic book, but most experienced travel photographers will confirm that they should be. There is no point in getting paranoid about them, as the vast majority need never arise if the proper preparations are made, but unless you do take account of them you may simply be storing up trouble for yourself.

The problems arise at several times, and with several different groups of people. Broadly, the likeliest areas of difficulty are when you leave your own country; when you arrive at your destination; when you are actually taking the pictures; when you leave; and when you return to your own country. A cynic might observe that this covers most of the trip, but it is not really so: once you have arrived, you are only ever likely to be challenged (if at all) when you take a picture of a sensitive subject. The trick lies in knowing what constitutes a sensitive subject.

In order to leave your own country, you are likely to need a valid passport with (if applicable) a visa or visas for the places you are going to visit. Getting these is, of course, your responsibility, but two pieces of advice are in order for those who have never done this before. First, apply for your passport well in advance of your intended trip – they can take an amazingly long time to arrive – and secondly, check out the visa requirements *very* carefully. Check which countries require a visa, whether it costs anything, what forms you have to fill in, whether you need to supply any additional passport-sized pictures, how long it will take, and how long it entitles you to stay in the country. Apply well in advance, and check progress at intervals if things take longer than they should. Finally, remember that everyone else in your party will be subject to similar rules, so make sure that they are prepared too.

You will very rarely have any trouble with customs as you *leave* a country, unless there are restrictions on currency export or on some reasonably common item of commerce such as ivory. What you may find a trial is the security at major airports.

Let there be no mistake: X-rays can and do damage unexposed and exposed film. If at all possible *insist* on hand inspection of films. You are likely to find this easier if you can carry the films in your hand as you pass through the security gate; some people pack all their film in a clear plastic bag so that it can be withdrawn from the gadget-bag and inspected

separately whilst the bag is X-rayed, but this does mean risking any film you have in the camera. Ideally, you should go through with an empty camera anyway – this lets the security guard root about inside, and keeps him happy – so it need not be too much of a problem.

A useful tip is to strip off the outer cartons from 35mm film, so that all you are carrying is the tubular plastic canister. Tape the end of the film-box to the outside of the canister for identification. This has four great advantages: first, it makes the film easier to pack; secondly, it speeds up inspection (especially if the security guard decides to inspect each canister in turn, which I have heard of happening); thirdly, it helps persuade the customs at the other end that the film is not for resale; and finally, it is a lot more convenient and litter-free when you are changing films in the field.

On arrival at the other end, your first hurdle is immigration. If your papers are in order, this is very rarely a problem. As well as the passport, some countries may demand certificates of vaccination; check this when you get your visa. The only countries which will normally give you a rough time are those with an illegal immigrant problem.

There is another matter which may be under the aegis of either immigration or customs. Some countries have been suffering from infestations of hippies, and will therefore insist that you have either a return ticket (or 'ticket out') or plenty of money – sometimes both. A few countries will even insist on set sums, perhaps so much per day plus a fixed amount. In practice, you are unlikely to be investigated on this score unless you look like a bad risk.

At customs, the investigating officer's business is to make sure that you are not importing equipment for resale. In a poor country, an affluent Western photographer's equipment may be literally incredible to an official whose annual salary could not pay for it; understandably, he may suspect that you are importing it for resale. The same goes for film.

To make matters worse, many countries have customs regulations rooted firmly in the nineteenth century. It is by no means unusual to find such restrictions as 'two cameras, and twenty-four plates or ten rolls of film'.

Once again, the practice may be very different from the theory, but it is as well to keep your equipment to a minimum when you are travelling, for this reason as much as for any other. If you do go significantly over the limit, it may be advisable to point this out at customs; I have always found that if you are honest and open, customs officials are prepared to ignore what might be called 'reasonable' transgressions. If, on the other hand, you try to smuggle stuff in, they can throw some very weighty penalties at you.

Two things which are always worth doing are listing all your equipment (with serial numbers, where applicable) and film on a sheet of paper, and dividing the equipment (at least nominally) among the members of the party. The former is invaluable if the customs officer wants a list of gear – some countries will enter it in your passport, to make sure you take it out again – and very useful both as a checklist and in case of theft. The latter provides an easy and legal way of getting around limitations: for example, a party of three can carry six cameras if the limit per person is two.

Once you are in the country, you are unlikely to be troubled again unless, as I have already mentioned, you try to photograph 'sensitive' subjects. In almost any country, this will include obvious military installations; even if it does not, there is always the chance that some bored military policeman will run you in, and if you are a foreigner you can look forward to making a long and tiresome series of explanations. Naval dockyards, military airfields, and (to a lesser extent) army camps are not the best subjects to choose.

The difficulty arises when the government has a wider view of 'military' or 'strategic' than you do. For example, many Communist countries regard all airfields as potentially military, and some will object to pictures of dams and bridges. The really repressive ones even class roads as of strategic importance, though few go so far as one African country – I forget which one – which banned the taking of any photographs without a permit. If you have any doubts, check them out with the relevant embassy – and remember that not every embassy official can be relied upon to give a straight answer. Check again if you are still unsure and (preferably) get permission in writing.

Whilst it is almost impossible to get official written letters from embassies and travel bureaux, what you often can get is some form of official leaflet which will answer most or all of your questions. Because they are standard tourist information leaflets, they are easy to get – just ring the National Tourist Office for the country concerned and they will send them along, often with a map and other useful tourist information. It is not a bad idea to carry the leaflet with you, in case of arguments with local officials who are either working to out-of-date information or who have their own ego-assertion problems.

Remember that even if the subject of your picture has absolutely no strategic, military, political, or any other importance, there may still be people with legitimate or illegitimate interests in stopping you photographing it. There is a story of one person who photographed the Bank of England in London, and who was then questioned by the Metropolitan Police because they thought he might have been gathering information for a break-in – though it is a very old story. As for illegitimate interests, it is as well to be very careful when photographing any kind of political demonstration or rally, since some of the participants may well take exception to being photographed.

You should also take due note of local regulations and customs. For example, many public places forbid the use of a tripod, even if photography is permitted, and many museums and art galleries make a small charge for a photography permit. In Islamic countries, as already mentioned, people may object to having their pictures taken; and if you are roughed up and your camera broken, you may find the police strangely unsympathetic. Besides, unless you speak the language, you may have some difficulty in explaining that your assailant, and not you, is the one at fault.

When it comes to leaving the country, you are unlikely to run into any problems unless you are trying to export a forbidden item – new ivory from India, say, or certain antiques of great value from England – or have managed to sell or lose any of the equipment recorded in your passport, if this was done on entry. In case of theft, *always* report it to the police *immediately* – it may be more trouble than the item is worth, but it will save you the double indignity of having to pay tax on it as well. Such taxes can be punitive, too – in India, at one time, they stood as 155% of value.

On return to your country, immigration officials are seldom a problem. Sometimes, they may require vaccination certificates if you have come from an area known to be in the grip of an epidemic, but usually they will just wave you through.

Customs are another matter. If you are carrying new or mint cameras, they may well demand proof that you have not bought them abroad. About the only way to furnish this is to have receipts (or, for more security, photocopies of the receipts) with you. I have never had any difficulty whatsoever with customs on my return to England, perhaps because of my honest face or because of the obviously well-used nature of my gear, but some people have: the receipts are a simple precaution, and one worth taking.

After all this catalogue of potential catastrophes, it may look as if the game is not worth the candle. Despite appearances, this is simply not true. It is impossible to overemphasise that in all probability, you will have absolutely no difficulties whatsoever on your trip. Even professional photographers, with huge quantities of equipment, films, and what looks like a travelling harem of models seldom have any problems, and as a private traveller the chances are vanishingly small. But they are only vanishingly small if you have taken the right precautions. Otherwise, you will have no trouble ninety-nine times out of a hundred – but on the hundredth...

TOWNS AND CITIES

'Faraway places, with strange-sounding names...' It may be a corny old song, but it still has the ring of truth about it. There is something in the very idea of foreign parts which is inescapably romantic, and translating your feelings into pictures is what photography is all about.

It is probably impossible to go anywhere with completely neutral feelings. Everywhere has an image, compounded of the books we have read, the pictures we have seen, the people we have met or heard, and of still subtler and less definable materials. Sometimes, the image will chime perfectly with the actuality; for example, Bermuda was almost exactly what I had expected. At other times, image and reality will be very different – but the tension resulting from the difference can be turned to creative advantage.

Because of this essential duality of vision – preconception and reality, or belief and experience – there are many ways to photograph a place. It is not simply that there are many subjects, and that you can select those subjects in different ways; it is that there are different kinds of seeing. If this seems impossibly mystical, bear with me for a while.

First of all, there is what one might call the 'consensus' approach. As a caricature, Paris consists entirely of the Eiffel Tower and the Champs Élysées, and is peopled with men who wear berets and ride bicycles, and impossibly elegant women. Whilst this is obviously untrue, it does reflect all our visual prejudices about France: if you add in a shop selling frogs' legs, a pavement cafe, and a cast-iron *pissoir*, the picture is complete.

Such pictures should not be despised. They provide what the movie industry calls 'establishing shots', setting the scene, providing a background, and telling you where you are. Even to the most insensitive, they will conjure up a set of feelings, perhaps of memories, and in doing so they tell far more than they show.

What is difficult about the establishing shot is that it has already been done very many times, and often by highly-skilled photographers; unless our own results are first class they invite unfavourable comparison with what has gone before.

It is, of course, quite possible to ignore all the old standards, and to concentrate on taking other types of picture. By doing so, though, the chances of presenting a coherent and complete picture of the subject are much decreased: Paris without the Eiffel Tower is simply not Paris as far as many people are concerned. If you are only concerned with single images, this is not particularly important, but if you are trying to put together an audio-visual sequence you are handicapping yourself very badly.

There are several ways to attack the 'old faithfuls'. One of the easiest is to take your tripod and take a night shot. Whilst this may be seen as a bit of a cop-out, it can get you out of trouble and even result in a picture which is genuinely different and worthwhile; for example, Notre Dame is extremely difficult to render well by day, but when it is lit with an eerie orange glow at night it is possible to get some absolutely superb and still perfectly recognisable pictures.

Another possibility is to lift the picture out of the ordinary by some piece of optical trickery. An old favourite is the ultra-wideangle shot (say 21mm on 35mm), or even a fish-eye, and lately the burgeoning of filter systems has given another option. 'Gradual' filters are one possibility, whilst others are multi-image and starburst; the latter work particularly well at night.

The trouble with this approach is that it is easy to fool yourself into thinking that something is original when in fact it is merely different. A boring picture with a straight-from-the catalogue effect on it is likely still to be boring; you need to be both critical and inventive in how you use the filter (or whatever) if the picture really is to be worthwhile.

Another alternative is to use the 'old faithful' landmark simply as a background. You can do this in all sorts of ways. A professional solution might be to have a couple of lovers walking hand-in-hand down the Champs Élysées, with the Arc de Triomphe in the background. You are breaking one of the generally-accepted rules of composition by having two principal subjects – the lovers and the arch – but because there are people in the picture, the eye will normally go to them first and the Arc de Triomphe will be noticed almost subliminally. Alternatives to the lovers might include some elegant lady with her Parisian pooch; if you want to introduce a note of humour, wait until he cocks his leg against a lamppost... Again, last time I was in Paris, the roller-skate craze was at its height. By going up into the Trocadéro gardens, I had a ready-made and very attractive foreground to the Eiffel Tower in the form of skilled and often beautiful teenage roller-skaters.

Often it is possible to show your 'old faithful' as a reflection. Mirrored sunglasses have been used so often as to approach cliché status, and in any case you really need a beautiful girl to wear them, but you can try automobiles – polished paintwork, windows, or hubcaps – shopfronts, puddles...exercise your ingenuity. Sometimes, you may be able to get away with nothing more than a shadow; the Eiffel Tower sounds like a good candidate for this treatment, though I must confess that I have never tried it.

Yet another possibility is to show rather more of the foreground and surroundings than is normally seen – how often does a photograph show the surroundings of the Taj

Mahal, for example? Showing an evening traffic-jam on the Champs Élysées not only gets your establishing shot in; it also raises something of a smile of sympathy for the French commuter from his English (or American, or whatever) counterpart.

Sometimes, you can strike lucky – though if you plan carefully, it is surprising how much 'luckier' you will get. Snow, for example, is almost always attractive. Sometimes it can be something of a novelty – when did you last see a picture of the Eiffel Tower under snow? – and even when we expect it, as in Russia's Red Square, it still improves the picture. To get good pictures of unspoiled snow, you will need to get up at dawn, and even then you may be too late in a busy city.

Other 'lucky' shots include parades in front of the landmark; flags and bunting tied to it for some festival; perhaps a *son et lumière* performance. If there are trees, remember the buds of spring and the reds and golds of fall as counterfoils to the picture.

You can even take the bull by the horns and try for a 'straight' shot. Use the work of other photographers (particularly in picture postcards) as a guide both to possibilities and things to avoid. Set the camera up on a tripod, use a polarising filter to get the maximum blue in the sky, and away you go.

There are many, many other possibilities, ranging from hiring batteries of lights and illuminating the subject to suit your own taste, to showing one of those little paperweight Eiffel Towers instead of the real thing; you still have your establishing shot, and you have something undeniably different. If you are making a tape-slide presentation, do not forget the possibility of using sound: either voice-over or appropriate music, such as accordions for the French or sitar ragas for India.

So much for the 'consensus' style of photography. Whilst it may be amusing to shoot only 'typical' pictures, it is also limiting and can prove to be too heavy a diet: what it needs is something lighter.

This is provided by the 'as is' approach. Now, whilst this is ostensibly objective, it actually depends on the photographer's own reaction to a place. For example, in India, one photographer might concentrate on the temples and ruins; another might choose the hurly-burly of the bazaar; and a third might be struck by the poverty and the abundance of beggars. Each of these 'is' India, but none of them could claim to be a complete picture.

What you have to do for this sort of photograph is to acknowledge your bias, and make allowance for it. By all means let it colour your perception, so that it is a thread running through your work, but be aware that there is more to the subject than that.

To begin with, there are what might be called the minor establishing shots. There are the pictures which will evoke a sigh of recognition from those who know the place, and will give some insight into it to those who do not. To return to Paris, for instance, there is that curious system of street-cleaning which reverse-flushes the drains, so that cool and (relatively) clean water wells up from them and sluices through the gutters; there are the shops and advertisements, including such typically Parisian sights as the shellfish stalls and the *boucheries chevalines*; the anarchic parking; the graffiti; the flyposting; the Algerian food shops; the picnickers beside the Seine.

After this, it is a question of personal vision. For instance, you might be struck (not literally, one hopes) by the insouciant style of driving, which results in so many dented cars. If you could find such a scene, it would be very rewarding to photograph the altercation which followed one of those minor collisions, complete with much arm-waving and yelling of Gallic insults.

One of the things which always fascinates me is the people in the sidewalk cafes, especially those extroverts who sit outside and indulge in theatrically intense conversations over black coffee. At night, the pictures can be even more fascinating; on the Boulevard St Michel, there are strolling players, Algerian vendors of knick-knacks, American students drunk on Paris, mysterious characters in raincoats like something out of a thriller movie – the list is endless, but we shall return to photographing people later.

Moving on from the 'as is' approach, we come to what I call the 'novel' approach. This seeks to show people the things they did *not* know about the place, or the things which they half-know but never think about. For example, there are the legions of cats which dwell in any city; the junk-shops, each with its own peculiar local flavour; perhaps the seedier side of the nightlife. Often, you can catch even natives unawares: many New Yorkers are unaware of the city's remarkable number of Victorian buildings, and there are innumerable Angelenos who have never seen the Watts Towers.

This way of taking photographs implies two things: a fairly high degree of specialisation and a modest amount of research. In a sense, the two are inseparable, because you will never discover the novelties without a bit of research and you will never need to do the research unless you want to specialise.

This is as good a point as any to mention the inherent paradox necessary in travel photography. You must live by two opposing rules: first, that of building upon what you know, and secondly, that of being open to experiment.

You have to build on what you know, because the means of taking good pictures does not change simply because you are in another country. Apart from the usual technical skills of correct exposure and so forth, there is the question of how you are accustomed to use those skills. To take a simple example, I could judge night-time exposures even without an exposure meter, because I do a lot of low-light photography. Another photographer, however, might be lost in the same circumstances; but could, say, judge the correct exposure compensation to apply when photographing a single dew-sparkled flower-head without thinking, whereas I would have to stop and think about the effect that I wanted. Each photographer's skills are honed by what he likes doing, and does best.

On the other hand, you have to be open to experiment precisely because you are abroad. For example, I do very little landscape photography in England, because the part of the countryside where I live is not the kind of countryside I like to photograph: but in the Austrian Tyrol, or the Himalayas, where there are the mountains that I love, I devote long periods to landscape work. In Los Angeles, my other base, I pursue an intermediate course: every now and then I will announce to my wife that I am going to 'do an Ansel Adams', and we will set off up the Pacific Coast Highway with a large format camera.

In real life, the paradox hardly exists at all as a paradox; there is no tension between conservatism and, experiment, because each draws upon the other and renews and refreshes the other. It is as well, though, to be aware of it. Otherwise, you can easily fall into the trap of assuming that merely because you can take *this* sort of photograph, you can also take *that* sort of photograph; and it ain't necessarily so.

At its extreme, the 'novel' approach ceases merely to be novel and becomes perverse. What happens here is that the common experience – the image which everyone else has of the place, including its more recherché parts – is subordinated to the unusual, the bizarre, and – I use the word again – the perverse.

In one way, this can be very interesting. If you seek out the backstreets, the decaying ruins, the criminal and near-criminal areas, the vagabonds, and so forth, you may well be showing people something about which they know nothing and ought, perhaps, to know something. The tiresome side, though, comes when you show something which has already been shown a thousand times, which everyone knows about, and which is simply unattractive.

Here, it may seem that I am being heartless, and that I am decrying crusading photojournalism (which is what this tends to become). I am not. What I am objecting to is *bad* crusading photojournalism. It is the hallmark of good crusading photojournalism that it wakes people up and makes them do something; the bad variety simply bores them still more by repetition of something which they already dislike. The first time that you see the poverty of an Indian city, or the first time you witness the repression of Indian women even in the United Kingdom, you want to yell and tell everyone about it. Unless you can do that in a powerful and original way, you are harming your cause more than advancing it, and would do better to start collecting coins on a street corner for Oxfam or some other charity.

There is another negative aspect to this sort of work. Whilst I would not advocate a Disneyland-like picture in which there is no crime, no poverty, no ugliness, no abuse of drugs or sex, I do query the wisdom of constantly harping on the dismal side of things; maybe the world could be a better place, but it does have its good points.

Finally, there is yet another approach. Unlike the others, it makes no attempt to 'tell it like it is'. The pictures are purely personal ones. They may be as lightweight as a picture of the hotel where you stayed, the bar where you had a drink, the crowded state of the beach. They may be high-flown abstracts, distillations of your experience as you experienced it, perhaps unrecognisable as a particular place. They may be almost anything.

Whilst many of these pictures will be so private as to be only personal *aides-mémoire*, you may yet find that others are the most telling of the entire trip. It is often impossible to know at the time; but these pictures which come straight from the heart may well surprise you.

PEOPLE

Whilst few of us feel any reservations about photographing, say, Red Square in Moscow or Trafalgar Square in London, most will have some scruples about poking a camera into someone's face and taking a picture.

This is not only a natural reaction, but also (I suggest) a desirable one. Turn it around: how would you feel if a total stranger leaned over your back fence and photographed you whilst you were having a barbecue or reading the Sunday papers?

Any photograph of a person involves some invasion of privacy. It may be trivial – no-one would object to being a passer-by in a picture of a famous landmark, for example – or it may be quite considerable: at the extreme, you may actually be inside their house. The photographer's job is to make that invasion as minor as possible, or even to make it enjoyable for the subject.

Before going on to how this is done, there is an important point to make. In almost every country in the world, it is perfectly legal to take a picture of someone in a public place, or a place to which the public has access. It is also normally quite legal to exhibit that picture if it does not 'hold the subject up to ridicule or contempt', or some such phrase – and the courts will normally take quite a robust view of this, so the picture has to be pretty defamatory for any action to lie. What is most assuredly not legal in most countries is to use that picture for any sort of advertising or even (in some places) commercial publication.

If you want to use someone's picture commercially, you will normally need a *model release*. This is a contract, signed by the person in the picture (or by a parent or guardian if the subject is under the age of contractual majority), which allows you to do pretty much what you like with the photograph. Because it is a contract, most legal systems will insist that it be made for 'valuable consideration', which can be anything from a penny to a very considerable model fee. It need not even be in cash: consideration in kind, such as a copy of the picture or a trip to Disneyland, will suffice.

The travel photographer is rarely troubled by this. In the first place, the chance of his subject ever seeing the picture is remote; in the second place, the likelihood of a successful action being brought internationally is not high; and in the third place, *most* countries and states (though not all) will only countenance such an action if the subject has suffered damage or loss in some way. This damage or loss, though, can include damage to reputation or loss of the earnings they might have made if they had been paid a modelling fee.

I do not know of any travel photographer who has been troubled by an international suit, but I do know one very pressing story about a photograph taken in the United States of a water-skier. It was used, without the skier's permission, in an advertisement in one of the men's magazines – *Playboy* or *Penthouse* or something similar – and he (being a pillar of the Church) sued. Successfully. For a lot of money. The moral of this tale is to be very careful about advertising use; I do not think that any other use (ie editorial) would ever lead to any trouble, but in (for example) New York State or California I would advise you to check with your lawyer.

Now, to return to the matter of actually taking pictures. There are four rough divisions into which such pictures fall: street pictures (including public places in general); work; play; and home. Each has its own particular techniques.

Street pictures covers a considerable spectrum, from people who might reasonably expect to be photographed to people who are simply going about their everyday business. The first category includes the gorgeously uniformed guards outside, say Horseguards Parade, or even the policeman outside No. 10 Downing Street, plus such pieces of street theatre as hot gospellers, street musicians and artists, and hot-chestnut sellers.

Some of these can scarcely object to being photographed. The guards, for example, are acknowledged tourist bait. Others, however, may complain.

As far as I am concerned, hot gospellers and political activists have no cause for complaint whatsoever. They are out to be noticed, and if the person who notices them happens to have a camera – well, so what? The only difficulty that can arise is if they happen to have their audience with them, and the audience turns upon the photographer. This is unlikely, and is in any case usually easy to detect; but it is as well to remember that if the proceedings are in a language which you do not speak, you can run into problems quite quickly and easily if things do turn nasty – a point to remember in all street photography.

Similarly, hot-chestnut sellers, pretzel-vendors, and flower-sellers have little cause for complaint – though some gypsy flower-sellers still seem to believe in the 'evil eye', and object violently to having their picture taken. As for those who are touting for money, such as buskers, pavement artists, and the Hare Krishna brigade, it seems only fair to put a coin or two in their collecting box in exchange for the picture. Most will smile at that, but a few may object.

As for the general public, that is another matter. Almost by definition, the pictures which attract us are the people who are out of the ordinary: the tramps, the vivid punks, the *filles de joie*, the eccentrics. Equally by definition, they are the ones who are least conventional and least inclined to follow the custom of politely ignoring people. A particular problem arises with beggars: obviously, it is as well to give them a little money, but the likelihood then is that they will try to wring some more out of you or (especially in India) that hordes more will materialise as if from nowhere and they will all have their hands out. You will not even be able to photograph them in many cases, as you will be so jostled, hassled, and (possibly) pick-pocketed that flight is the only possibility.

As often as not, though, a smile and a gesture which says, 'May I take your picture?' (half-raising the camera will usually do) will bring willing cooperation. If you do get a smile of agreement, you may also get a deliberate 'pose'. The best way around this is to take one picture, and then to fiddle with the camera until they lose interest; then, take the picture you wanted. One expression which is well worth learning, in any language, is 'thank you'.

If you do not get willing cooperation, either forget it or weigh your chances of escaping. If you want the picture badly enough, take it and run – but remember that in some cases (particularly gangs of youths and ladies of the night) there may be other people around to block your escape.

Another problem you may encounter from time to time is that of the person who wants some money for being photographed. This is particularly rife in Kathmandu, but it can happen a lot nearer home. I remember one exceptionally picturesque old gentleman who used to sit on a street-corner in Sandys parish of Bermuda; it was said that he made a regular fortune from being photographed, sitting, picturesque as you please, until the picture had been taken and then pursuing the hapless tourist and demanding money.

I have mixed feelings about this. On the one hand, you can hardly blame a poor person for asking for a few coins from a rich one, especially when the rich one has (in however small a way) taken advantage of him; and equally, it must be a bit tough to sit in your favourite place in the sun and be forever interrupted by tourists with cameras. On the other hand, the wholesale dispensation of *baksheesh* to everyone whose picture you take is both expensive and inconsiderate to other photographers, quite apart from any effect it may have on the subject. If I photograph anyone who is obviously a beggar, or at least very poor even by the standards of the society in which he lives, then I will give him a few coins; otherwise, no.

In order to minimise the likelihood of being noticed, some photographers like to use longer-than-normal lenses, say 90mm or 105mm; some even favour 135mm or 200mm. Still others use 'angle-scopes', 45° mirrors built into oversize lenshoods so that the picture is taken at right angles to the line of apparent sight.

As far as I am concerned, the only time when 'sneak shots' are justified (if they ever are) is when it is impossible to get a picture any other way – as, for example, in some of the more fanatically Muslim countries. The best solutions then are either the unaimed shot, or the use of the twin-lens reflex.

In either case, the camera must be pre-set. Use a small stop – the smallest you can whilst still retaining a reasonable shutter-speed – and pre-set the distance to roughly what will be needed: depth of field will take care of the rest. On a 35mm camera, consider a wide-angle lens.

With a little experience, it is quite possible to aim a camera remarkably accurately without looking through the viewfinder. This technique is best with black-and-white, as composition can be 'trued up' in the enlarger afterwards, but it can also be used with colour slides if masks are used in mounting for projection. Press the shutter release as casually as possible, and do not immediately start to fiddle with the camera. A Leica or other non-reflex is best, as the shutter is far quieter than the slam-bang of a mirror in a reflex.

The TLR, being used at waist-level, is far less obtrusive than any eye-level camera; it can also be held with a lens pointing to left or right, instead of ahead. A quick glance into the finder, and press the button. The shutter is very quiet, and the chances of detection are small, especially if you are photographing people unused to cameras. It is possible to use an SLR with waist-level finder in the same way, but then you have the noise to contend with.

So far, we have really only been concerned with pictures in passing. Only rarely are you likely to be involved in conversation with your subject. When we move on to people at work, though, we are talking about gaining access to their place of work – unless, of course, they work in the street.

In gaining access, you have to deal with people at different levels. Unless the person doing the work is also the proprietor, you will need to get the proprietor's permission; and if there is another, intermediate, level you will have to speak to the supervisor, foreman, floor manager, etc. Unless you are on good terms with *everyone*, at all levels, you are unlikely to do at all well. How you go about this depends on you, but you can be surprisingly successful if you just walk into the general office and explain what you want to do. You will have to have a reasonable command of the language, and it is as well to have a convincing reason ready, but you can get a lot done this way. Better still is a letter to the place in question before you leave, or a personal introduction from someone on the spot.

Once you are in, you have two separate things to think about. One is not getting in the way, which is only common sense and common courtesy, and the other is how to show what is going on.

The latter may not be as easy as it sounds. Presumably, the reason you are there is that it is unique, or at least unusual; an ordinary machine shop, for example, you could photograph as well (and a lot more easily) in your own country.

Incidentally, it is as well never to use flash for this sort of picture; it is not only distracting for your subject (and even dangerous, in some instances), but it also destroys the atmosphere in the vast majority of cases. You may need fast lenses, and fast film as well; the ideal, I have found, is a 35mm f/1.4 with Kodachrome 64, but if you are prepared to put up with slightly worse grain you can try 200 ASA film, possibly pushed to 400 ASA. A 64 ASA film at f/1.4 is the same as a 200 ASA film at f/2.5 or 400 ASA at f/3.5. With rollfilm, I use the lens wide open (f/2.8) and push 200 ASA ED to 250 ASA or so. The same is true for grab shots in public places indoors.

Even now, your interaction with your subject is likely to be fairly simple and straightforward – the occasional question about the work (and compliment on its quality) – and it is quite clear why you are there. Taking pictures of people at play is another matter.

There are some places, such as fairgrounds, where people seem to take it as entirely normal that they should be photographed. In others, they feel their privacy a bit more keenly: on some beaches, for example, the photographer is likely to be signally unwelcome. This is especially true, I am told, of nudist beaches.

In such circumstances, you are much more likely to have to give some account of yourself, partly because people wonder why you are photographing them and partly because they have more time to wonder. When they are walking in the street, or working, or even looking at pictures in an art gallery or reading a newspaper, they may be too preoccupied to notice you and too interested in what they are doing to comment if they do. If they are relaxing, though, they have the time to ask.

I have always found that it is better to stop and talk than to hurry away. At the very least, it makes life more agreeable for all parties, instead of engendering suspicion, and at best it can actually lead you on to even more interesting pictures. I remember on one occasion being stopped by a monk in Dharamsala and asked what we were doing; by the time I had finished explaining, we had been invited up to his monastery, a small *puja* or rite had been arranged for us to photograph, and one of the senior monks had been asked to do a *mho* or prediction for the success of the book we were writing.

The reason for this is simply that people are, in general, helpful and interested in other people. One might also suspect that they are flattered that you find them so interesting; most people see their lives as fairly boring, and to have someone else take an interest reinforces their own good opinion of themselves.

One last point which is appropriate to this chapter concerns the photography of interiors, especially church and temple interiors. Often, you can only gain access to these by rooting out the person who has the key or by asking the Lord Abbot or whoever is in charge. In the former case, a small tip is usually quite sufficient; in the latter, I always like to give a Polaroid of the subject (it helps me to determine the exposure, too!) as well as a contribution to church funds. You have to be a bit careful about this, to make it clear that it is for the church, or you can give offence, but it is good policy.

LANDSCAPE

I never used to be very interested in landscape photography. Certainly, I admired the works of other photographers, but I could never really see what all the fuss was about. Most of all, I found it difficult to understand the time and effort which landscape photographers put into their work.

Admittedly, my own landscapes were never much good. I had some success in Bermuda, but that was mostly picture-postcard prettiness. I only really began to understand it when I first saw California.

Here, at last, was a place that I really wanted to photograph – and I couldn't. At least, not to my own satisfaction. I had years of experience in other kinds of photography; I had earned my living as a professional photographer; I had had one-man exhibitions; but I had never done any real, serious, out-in-the-country landscape work.

Some may find this amazing; was I not born in wild and beautiful Cornwall, where granite cliffs meet the Atlantic? It doesn't matter: there is something in mountains which makes me want to take landscape pictures. Since first I saw the Californian mountains, I have seen the Himalayas and the Alps, and the mountains of Spain and Northern Portugal, and my fascination with mountain landscapes has grown apace.

This biographical aside has two purposes. The first is to show how travel can quite suddenly awaken an interest in landscape photography where none has existed before. The second is to point out a fundamental truth of all photography, but one which is perhaps seen most clearly in landscape: you have to care about the subject, deeply and strongly, before you can begin to make good pictures of it.

After a while, you come to realise that it is more important to get the *right* picture than merely to get *a* picture. Think of your first attempts at capturing a landscape on film. The odds are that you were struck by the magnificence of a view, and you happened to have your camera with you. The picture may have looked all right in the viewfinder, when you were still intoxicated with the scenery around you, but it seemed curiously lifeless when it was reduced to a square of paper or plastic. If you were immediately satisfied, then either your standards were very low or you are a genius.

An immediate conclusion – perhaps whilst you were still looking through the viewfinder – may have been that the trouble lay in the camera's angle of view: you could see the whole panorama, whereas the camera abstracted a miserable rectangle. In most cases, though, fitting a wider lens makes things worse rather than better, as the wider you go, the more boring foreground there is and the smaller the principal subject looks.

Surprisingly, the most useful lenses for landscape are often those somewhat longer than usual: say, 100-200mm on 35mm, 150-250mm on rollfilm.

A second surprise is that there are very few successful landscapes without a principal subject, or centre of interest – centre in the artistic sense, not the mathematical. It need not be very much – a figure, a cottage, a lake, a waterfall – but it must be something that the eye can latch on to. Man has evolved with the instinct to look for things in a landscape – friends, enemies, shelter, food, water – and unless the eye can find this, it will roam unsatisfied over the picture.

This principal subject must stand out from the picture. People, and the works of man, stand out easily. So, for example, does the moon. But a mountain will not, unless it is isolated in one way or another: a row of mountains of more or less similar height simply raises the horizon.

The horizon, in turn, is very important. If it is too near the centre of the picture, it may simply chop the composition in half; if it is too near the top, the picture may seem oppressive, and if it is too near the bottom the result may be 'twee' and arty, but still ineffective.

The third point is no surprise. It is that you must have the final scale of the picture in mind when you take it. For example, if there is a huge mountain with a tiny house on the side, you must print the picture large enough for the tiny house to be seen. If, on the other hand, you have made a simple composition from a vast mountain, the blue evening sky, and the moon, it may be an image of such graphic strength that it is perfectly effective even at 24x36mm.

Finally, remember that all the time-worn concepts of 'rules of composition' were mostly formulated on the basis of landscape. I will not bore you by repeating them all here, but it is worth remembering that some of them have some validity. The 'rule of thirds', for example, states that if you mentally divide a scene into thirds, vertically and horizontally, by superimposing a noughts-and-crosses (tic-tac-toe) board on it, the intersections are often a good place to put your principal subject.

Similarly, the idea of the 'S-curve' (known to its detractors as the S-bend) is that a receding curve such as a river or a path can lead the eye into the picture. There is also the concept of balance (not making your picture one-sided, but treating it as if it were a pair of scales) and of tension, which says that straight lines (especially vertical or diagonal ones) are active or aggressive, whereas curved lines (especially long and roughly horizontal ones) are restful.

Taken to excess, these 'rules' result in sterile, though often modestly pleasant, pictures; used with restraint, or broken deliberately, they can be of considerable use.

Much more useful, though, is the cultivation of the particular state of mind. Zen Buddhists call it 'no mind', which may seem a little cryptic, and the Tibetan term translates as 'perfect appropriateness', which may not seem much clearer, but the concept is simple enough. Basically, it consists of waiting, of clearing the mind of preconceptions and distractions, and of trying to concentrate – perfectly – on the picture. When the moment is right, you press the button.

Unless you are blessed with a state of enlightenment, you are unlikely to be able to take pictures on this basis alone. What you can do, though, is spot the elements of a potential picture, and wait until they come together. This is not entirely a rational process, though obviously reason plays its part: you have to be able to operate the equipment. If ever you come across it, try reading Ansel Adams's account of how he took *Moonrise over Hernandez*; his story of everyone piling out of the pick-up, and furiously trying to set up the tripod and the big field camera, is most entertaining.

This capacity to wait is almost infinite in the case of the great landscape photographers. They will carefully pick a particular time of year, a particular time of day, when they know that the conditions are likely to be what they want: and then they wait. If the lighting is wrong, they will go away and return later – perhaps a year later. This is the sort of dedication great landscape photography demands.

Without aspiring to the status of Ansel Adams, though, we can still exercise a modicum of patience, and the results will more than justify the wait.

The other 'secret' of landscape photography is not to be afraid of a bit of leg-work. Tempting as it may be to hop out of the car, take a picture, and hop back in again, it is very unlikely indeed to be successful. Even a modest amount of walking about will pay great dividends, and if you are prepared to scramble up or down the odd goat-path, matters are likely to improve still more. Within reason, looking down is likely to prove more useful than looking up; but always be alive to the possibilities of both.

Before going on to a brief summary of the technical requirements of landscape work, there is one more thing to say. Everything I have said so far about landscape photography can be ignored.

I mean this only in the sense that there are plenty of perfectly successful landscape pictures made on the spur of the moment; with no principal subject; using a wide-angle lens; and completely ignoring all the rules of composition. Many of them work because of their use of colour, as may be seen from the illustrations, but others defy any such rational explanation: they just work. Just one word of warning: it helps if you have luck, or genius, or both, on your side for this sort of picture.

Apart from the selection of lenses, as already mentioned, the technical side of landscape photography is not particularly difficult. Serious landscape photographers mostly use medium or large format cameras to capture the range of tones and textures in a landscape. Equally important, they tend to use contrasty lenses: aerial haze can be a real nuisance in some pictures, though it adds to the mood of others. Zooms, with (in most cases) poor resolution and even worse contrast, are likely to prove very disappointing. A slight warming filter (81A) will reduce haze to some degree; a pale blue one will increase it.

Exposure determination is not as easy as it looks, especially if the sky is partly cloudy. Usually, incident light readings from the camera position will provide a better idea than reflected light readings, but you may well wish to depart from the meter's recommendation in order to get a particular effect. Underexpose for more saturation: overexpose for an ethereal effect, but watch out for pale skies.

Use a tripod whenever possible: it will improve camera steadiness (especially if you have been scrambling up the aforementioned goat-paths) and it also makes life easier if you do have to wait for a few minutes: you can set the camera up, and just wait until the light is right. If you have to hold the camera, the temptation is to get the picture over and done with, and move on.

Do not expect instant success. Landscape photography can be very rewarding – but it demands a lot. If you care enough about your subject, you will eventually begin to get it right.

NATURE

Unlike landscape photography, the desire to take up nature photography seldom springs upon someone simply as a result of travel. More often, the interest in photographing (say) insects, or birds, or nocturnal animals is gained at home, and its exercise when travelling is merely an extension of techniques already known.

There are, however, three relatively common exceptions to this, and one rider which applies to all nature photography away from home ground. The rider is a simple one: remember that you are dealing with a more or less different fauna from that encountered at home, which may harbour dangers which you do not appreciate.

For example, the English insect photographer can creep about in the undergrowth without much fear of what may lurk therein. In southern Europe, he may disturb scorpions; in Africa, snakes; in Australia, the Black Widow spider, and so forth. Furthermore, the photographer who has no experience of large and potentially dangerous animals should never underestimate their speed of movement and ability to do harm.

These dangers are (relatively) easily dealt with simply by taking care, and by listening to the advice of people who know what they are talking about – not those who think they know, who are much more frequently encountered, and who can be as dangerous as the perils you want to avoid.

The three exceptions are flowers, birds, and safari-type wildlife, by which I mean large animals which people used to shoot, but now mostly content themselves with photographing.

FLOWERS

Exotic flowers may prove an irresistible subject to the photographer who would never dream of photographing a flower in his garden. The commonest mistake is to try to photograph a whole bed or bush, in which case the result is normally a sea of green with a few spots of colour. In most cases, a single flower, spray of flowers, or (at most) bough is about all that can be encompassed.

Unless the flowers are truly gigantic, this inevitably means close-up photography. Most 35mm SLRs can focus close enough to handle the larger flowers, but anything smaller will require close-up apparatus. The cheapest and simplest, and optically the best, short of buying specially-designed lenses, is the humble dioptric close-up lens. Use the standard lens stopped down to f/5.6 or more, and the quality is likely to be excellent.

Special close-focusing micro lenses will give even better results and are much more convenient to use. A very few top-quality close-focusing zooms, notably the sadly discontinued 90-180mm f/4.5 Series 1 Vivitar, can also deliver excellent results; the majority of zooms are likely to be very soft indeed, though this may not matter all that much to you. The advantage of the longer focal lengths is that they give a greater working distance than the 50-55mm lens, though (contrary to common belief) depth of field is unaffected: it depends solely on the image magnification on the film. At, for example, half life size the depth of field will be the same whether you are using 55mm or 500mm.

Depth of field is likely to be a problem, and you may have to stop down considerably if you are photographing a flower such as a Hibiscus; with the smaller flowers, such as Tiara Tahiti, there is no difficulty. The trouble with stopping well down is that it implies long shutter speeds; and flowers will wave in the breeze. A reflector, such as the small Lastolite, is invaluable. Some photographers even use electronic flash, though I find that this is very difficult to do without creating an unnatural effect.

Try to keep the backgrounds simple. A plain, out-of-focus green, or the brown of the soil, is often best. Alternatively, choose a low angle and shoot against the sky – but in this case, remember to allow between one and three stops for the brightness of the sky, and stop down appropriately. Consider a polarising filter, both to saturate the colours of the flowers and to darken the sky. As usual, slight underexposure will result in more dramatic colours, but do not overdo it or the foliage will look unnaturally dark.

BIRDS

Most serious bird photographers rely heavily on hides, which allow them to get surprisingly close to their prey. Otherwise, you will have to use very long lenses. With a very few tame exceptions, small birds will require *at least* 300mm in most cases, and 500mm or 600mm is better if you have it. Larger birds, such as flamingos, may be possible with a 200mm. Even if you want to show groups of birds – flamingos again provide a good example – you are likely to need at least a 90 or 105mm lens.

Even an experienced bird photographer is inclined to shoot for the percentages, and accepts that many of his pictures may not be successful. If you really want to capture the fowl on film, use plenty of it.

BIG GAME

There are innumerable variables in this sort of photography, not least among which is how the animals are feeling that day. Typically, safari shots are taken from a Land Rover. With a skilled tracker-driver, and lots of luck, you may be able to get away with something like an 80-200mm zoom, but normally the 200mm end of the range will be what you are using. On the other hand, 500mm may well be too long for a lot of shots. If you are shooting from a vehicle, either keep the lens well away from the window-frames etc. and insulate it from vibration with your body, or turn the engine off and use the vehicle as a steady. Beware, though, of other passengers bouncing about inside!

If you decide to get your pictures the old-fashioned way, on foot, just remember how dangerous big game can be. You should really have an armed assistant whose job is to look out for any threats – *not* to concentrate on the photography.

In the excitement of big-game photography, it is easy to shoot wildly without any real thought. Not only does this result in bad pictures: it also means that nine times out of ten, you will miss the best pictures because you are reloading. Check your exposures carefully, remembering to make the appropriate adjustments for dark or (more usually) light

backgrounds, compose your pictures as best you can from a fixed viewpoint, and be selective about when you press the button. On the other hand, do not be afraid to bracket your exposures: for most people, safari photography is a once-in-a-lifetime experience, and it is foolish to try to save a few pennies on film.

RECORD PHOTOGRAPHY

In some types of expedition photography, the pictures are less important for their own sake than as raw data to be digested and processed when the expedition returns home.

For this sort of work, the criteria are completely different from other kinds of travel photography. Each type of expedition will have its own requirements, but the following observations should be generally applicable.

EQUIPMENT

The standard is 35mm, which can hold enough information for almost all applications; grain and lack of definition of fine textures are principally aesthetic drawbacks and are not usually important.

Because the camera may be used by people who are not particularly skilled photographers, an automatic exposure option is usually useful – though everyone should be given a brief explanation of how the auto-exposure system can be 'fooled' by high contrast and (especially) backlighting. It is useful also to have a manual option, so that those who do want to take more 'creative' pictures will not be unduly limited.

The single-lens reflex is easily the best design, as it is all but impossible to forget to focus. It should be a rugged model, as almost by definition this sort of expedition will be well off the beaten track, and it should be duplicated for safety's sake. A good plan is to take an electronic easy-to-use model, plus a basic old-fashioned mechanical camera as back-up. It is also as well to have two lenses – say 35mm and 50mm – in case of damage, loss, or the need to use two cameras at once.

Although flash has its problems, an automatic electronic flashgun (or two) can be extremely useful; the best solution may well be to take three or four relatively modest units, and regard them as expendable: when one packs up, unpack another. You will, of course, need plenty of batteries – another argument for guns of modest output. Remember that out-of-doors, or in mud huts or caves, the gun may well be operating at full power and that because less light will be reflected from floor, walls, and ceiling than envisaged by the manufacturer, the effective output will be reduced. The guide number may be reduced by 25-50%. In these conditions, manual guns may be a better bet.

Some expeditions swear by bulb guns using 'peanut'-sized bulbs. These are certainly very much simpler and more reliable than electronics, use fewer batteries, and give more light per flash; but you do need to carry an awful lot of bulbs.

A tripod is also very useful as a means of reducing flash consumption – just use longer exposures – but its principal use lies in providing a stable camera platform in a fixed place at a fixed height – very useful if comparative shots are to be taken or if camera-to-subject distance is to be measured accurately.

A data back can be invaluable for 'tagging' individual pictures; this makes recording information about each picture very much easier. An alternative is to use a front-of-lens data recording attachment.

Apart from such obvious pieces of equipment, it is a good idea to carry standard colour patches (available from Kodak). These are placed in shot, close to the subject, so that colour consistency can be checked; they are especially useful if photomechanical printing is envisaged, and virtually essential if colour print material is in use. An 18% neutral grey card will help printing and colour balancing. A cheap substitute in an emergency is a paint colour chart or similar colour swatch, but because these are not standardised they must be retained for comparison with the final picture.

Similarly, scaling measures are extremely useful as they show the size of the subject without the need for any external notes. Clear black-on-white scales are important; the size of the scale will obviously depend on the size of the subject. Folding carpenters' rules can be modified with a little paint for really large scales.

FILM

Transparency film is cheap, and if carefully processed gives repeatable 'accurate' colours. It is, however, critical of exposure and requires projection apparatus or a light table for viewing, which may not be convenient for raw data.

Colour print material is less critical of exposure, though exposure must be consistent if repeatable colours are required. If colour patches and an 18% grey card are included in the picture, a very high degree of colour repeatability is possible, but the custom printing required will be expensive. Convenience in viewing is, of course, very high.

Where colour is not important, black-and-white merits serious consideration. It is far more tolerant of inaccurate

exposure than colour film, and can be printed cheaply and easily. The inclusion of a standard grey scale, or even of an 18% grey card, will enable repeatable rendition of tone. Filters can be used to differentiate colours, if this is important: a given filter will lighten its own colour and darken its complementary colour.

EXPOSURE AND RECORDING

Colour patches, scales, etc., should be placed as close to the subject as possible and in the same plane as the subject. This ensures accurate scaling (which might otherwise be affected by the scale being nearer the camera than the subject, or vice versa) and in the case of colour means that the light falling on the colour patch is as near as possible to that falling on the subject.

It is normally essential to record extra information about each subject in a small notebook. Typically, this would include a brief description of the subject, date and time taken, the focal length of the lens, and the name of the photographer; you may also wish to include exposure details, plus any other special notes. The book should be filled in religiously at the time the pictures are taken. If this is not possible (for example, if one is at an awkward location or it is pouring with rain), it must be filled in as soon as possible, whilst everything is still fresh in the mind. Sometimes it is possible to record such data on a card or slate, in the picture, which can simplify matters considerably.

GENERAL

One person in the expedition should be responsible for the photography in general and the camera gear in particular. You may not wish to go to the lengths of signing gear in and out, but it should always be returned to the same person after use. This makes it easier to find when it is needed, and also increases the chances of its being looked after: if something is no-one's responsibility, then often no-one bothers to look after it.

Place all exposed film in the same place, so that it can be handed in for processing at once. Nothing is more irritating than finding you are missing a vital roll which then turns up (if at all) in someone else's kit.

Kodak supply an excellent leaflet, free of charge, on photography in the tropics. This covers risks to film and equipment, and although a little old-fashioned is well worth having.

Finally, check *everything* before you go, and make sure that everyone who will be using the equipment is familiar with it.

In addition to the obvious advantages, this means that any damage done by the ham-fisted is likely to be done whilst the gear is still repairable or replaceable, that any deficiencies in the equipment are shown up, and that you know that what you are doing is actually practicable.

PRESENTATION

The presentation of a single image is rarely a problem; it will normally be mounted as a print, and the style of the frame is a matter of personal taste, fashion, and the demands of the subject. It is important to note, though, that different pictures 'work' best at different sizes. For example, some are like miniature paintings on ivory; at quite small print sizes, they seem to glow with a jewel-like effect. Others require considerable enlargement to be seen at their best; for example, I have a weakness for tiny figures in huge landscapes – but if the final picture is less than about 8x10", the whole point of the picture is lost. Yet others will be perfectly acceptable over a wide range of print sizes – though excess magnification is something to be guarded against, as it reveals faults which would be invisible in smaller prints.

What we are concerned with here is the technique of presentation required to tell a complete story. This normally implies a whole series of pictures – the so-called 'picture essay' – though there have been a few pictures, such as those from the Farm Security Administration and some of Bert Hardy's war pictures, which seem to say everything in a single frame.

The picture essay is normally presented in one of three ways: in a book or magazine, as an exhibition of original prints, or as an audio-visual display. Each has its own requirements.

The book or magazine type generally consists of a very few pictures, rarely more than ten and possibly as few as three; anything more than ten, and the topic is beginning to approach book status in its own right. Except in photographic magazines, where people tend to linger oer the images, each picture must be direct, punchy, and tell its story immediately. This is not to say that it cannot consist of a wealth of detail, just that the principal subject must be immediately obvious.

In this approach, the pictures and the words which accompany them are mutually supportive, but the extent to which either is more important can vary enormously. In some cases, the pictures are mere incidentals to the text, no more than decoration; at the other extreme, a few words of captioning are all that is used. This is normally the preserve of professionals, and anyone who has tried this sort of work will see why.

The exhibition is another matter. Normally, there are far more pictures – twenty or thirty would be a reasonable sort of number – and the supporting role of words is minimal. The pictures must tell their own story almost unaided: the most that you can hope for is that the viewer will read a paragraph or two – at most one side of a single sheet of paper – and the captions under each picture.

Because the pictures in an exhibition are usually viewed by several people from a fair distance, it is normal that they should be fairly large. The exhibition will look very much better if they are all of the same size, or at least of very similar size, and are mounted in identical frames.

The frames need not be anything very special. Flush mounting on polystyrene boards is easy, but for extra protection you may wish to use glass: a chipboard backing and a few mirror clips can make a cheap but very effective frame.

Finally, the audio-visual presentation uses far more pictures than the exhibition – a common number is 80 or even 160 (a professional Carousel magazine holds 80 slides) and the pictures and the words or music can reinforce one another tremendously. Because there are so many pictures, it is usual to break the information down into bite-size pieces, and to have a single picture to illustrate each point. If, from time to time, you wish to present a more emotional or less specific sequence, music generally makes a better soundtrack than voice-over.

No picture in an audio-visual presentation should stay on the screen for too long; ten seconds would be the absolute maximum in normal use, with two to five seconds rather more usual. Because the pictures are only up for a brief time, they have to be very clear. They must, of course, be the right way up and the right way around – it is surprising how often this condition is not met, even in professional presentations, but it is easily arranged by running through the programme very briefly before its public showing.

The audio-visual is necessarily the most highly-structured of the three means of presentation, and this is true whether you are constructing some sophisticated multi-projector show, or just showing your holiday slides with an impromptu spoken commentary. Furthermore, because each slide is the centre of attention for the time it is on the screen, your commentary must be appropriate to it.

In fact, the approach to audio-visual presentations can with advantage be applied to the other methods of presentation as well, with due allowance for their differences; for example, with both the book and the exhibition, the reader/viewer can switch to and fro from text to picture, and return to an earlier picture if they feel the need – but they will be able to follow the flow much better if there *is* a flow.

The successful presentation – in whatever medium – begins long before the pictures are taken. Unless you plan the pictures you need, you are going to leave holes – possibly large and embarrassing holes – in the presentation. Some go to the lengths of a full shot list, but at the very least you need a list of the topics you are going to illustrate.

When it comes to the shooting, be sure that you cover all the subjects needed. Do not be afraid, though, to shoot extra pictures, as it is always possible for something new to come up which had not struck you before. If need be, make careful notes of the contents of the pictures, either at the time or whilst it is still fresh in your mind, as described earlier.

After the pictures have been processed, go through them carefully. Does any of them immediately strike you as summing up what you remember? If it does, it may be worth restructuring the original plan, and 'hanging' the presentation on that, especially if it is an exhibition. Try to use your best shots, but remember the need for an underlying structure, or 'angle'.

Throw out the bad pictures, unless they are absolutely essential for the meaning (and if they are that bad, ask yourself why). Also, throw out any duplicates or near duplicates, though you may occasionally be able to use these in audio-visual sequences either widely separated or to show the sequence of events at a particular time. Remember the waste-paper basket can be the photographer's greatest friend: if you only show your good shots, people will never know about your bad ones. Furthermore, it is better to leave your audience wishing for more, rather than wondering how much longer you are going to go on for.

Finally, decide on the final structure; the layout of the pictures in a picture essay (though this is usually someone else's responsibility), the order of pictures in an exhibition, the words, pictures, and music in an audio-visual or slide show. Put it together; in the case of an A-V, run it through. If you can, try it out on a test audience which can be constructively critical – preferably a friend who is not afraid to hurt your feelings, but who will not advise you to write if all off and start again. When the public see it you'll slay them in the aisles.

Monschau, Germany

▲ Tribesmen, Kenya

▲ Cab driver, New York City

▼ British Columbia, Canada

Hong Kong Harbour ▶

▼ Alkmaar cheese market, Holland

▲ Roadside scene, Mexico

New York City Police ▼

▲ Climbing for coconuts, Hawaii

Chinese dragon, Hong Kong ▼

35

The Atrium of the Citicorp Building, New York ▶

▲ Mountainside hut, Switzerland

▲ Selfridges department store, Oxford St, London

Windmills on the Greek Island of Mykonos ▼

Sunset on Sanur Beach, Bali, Indonesia ▼

▲ Gondolas, Venice

Waterloo Bridge, London ▼

Hansom cab in Central Park, New York ▶

▲ Monument Valley, Utah/Arizona

▲ Oakland Bay Bridge, San Francisco

▼ Brasilia, Brazil

Chinatown, San Francisco ▼

42

◀ Keukenhof flower exhibition, Holland

Leigh-on-Sea, Essex ▼

Statue of Liberty, Upper New York Bay ▶

▲ Greek villager

▲ Traditional Thai costumes

▲ Gondolier, Venice

Bullfight, Mexico City ▼

▼ Rialto Bridge, Venice

▲ Winter fun, Austria

▲ Fiesta, Mexico

▼ Snake charmer, India

▼ Carnival, Rio de Janeiro, Brazil

▲ Firth of Forth suspension bridge, Scotland

▲ Flags around the base of the Washington Memorial

▼ The Capitol, Washington

Eros, Piccadilly Circus, London ▶

▼ Chinese artist, Hong Kong

▲ Nelson's Column, Trafalgar Square, London

▲ The Buckingham Memorial Fountain, Chicago

▼ Hong Kong Harbour

The Statue of Liberty, New York ▶

▲ The northern waterfront, San Francisco

▲ Sunset, Cape Cod, Massachusetts

▼ Rice fields, Bali

▲ The Palace of Westminster, London

▼ Silhouette of Egyptian village li

◀ Canary Islands ▲ Paris ▼ Venice

▲ Caribbean carnival

▲ Scene in Henley during the Regatta

▼ Hispanic Parade, New York City

▲ Religious ceremony at the Wailing Wall, Jerusalem

▲ Roman spectator

▲ The Taj Mahal, India

▼ The domes of Santa Maria della Salute, Venice

▼ Hawaiian sunset

▲ Bryce Canyon, Utah

Delicate Arch in Arches National Park, Utah ▶

▲ The Great Glacier, Switzerland

▼ The Matterhorn, Switzerland

◄ Briksdalsbreen glacier, Norway   ▲ The Dhaulargiri glacier, Nepal   Mount Everest, Himalayas, Nepal ▼

◀ Mount Everest

▲ Mt Kilimanjaro, Tanzania

▲ The Nepalese mountains of the Gauesh Himal

▲ The Grand Tetons, Wyoming

57

▲ Dream Lake, Colorado

Mount Shuksan in North Cascades National Park, Washington ▶

◀ Rio de Janeiro, Brazil   ▲ Victoria Falls   ▼ Tississat Fa

Iguaçu Falls

Machu Picchu, Peru ▶

UNITED STATES OF AMERICA

▲ Disneyland

▼ Football, Atlanta

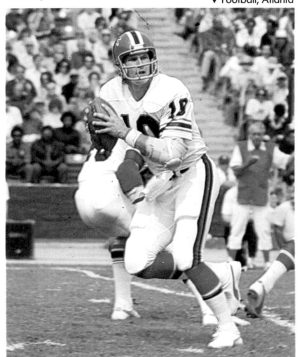

▼ Walt Disney World

▲ Jefferson Memorial

▼ Indians, Texas

▲ Lincoln Memorial

▼ Pageantry, Williamsburg, V

▲ Football, Atlanta, Georgia

LUNAR MODULE TEST ARTICLE
LTA-8

UNITE
STATE

▲ Lyndon B Johnson Space Center, Houston, Texas

63

◄ Burnham Park Yacht Harbor, Chicago, Illinois

▲ Houston, Texas

▲ Yale University, Connecticut

▲ Wiscasset, Maine

▲ Acadia National Park, Maine

▼ Pemaquid Lighthouse, Maine

▲ Provincetown, Massachusetts

▼ The Dwight-Barnard House, Deerfield, Massachusetts

▲ Oakland Bay Bridge, San Francisco

▲ Fisherman's Wharf, San Francisco

▲▼ San Francisco

▲ Chinatown

▼ Lombard Street, San Francisco

67

▲ Ruth Glacier on Mount McKinley, Alaska

Harris Beach State Park, Oregon ▶

▲ Midway Geyser Basin, Yellowstone National Park

▲ West Mitten, Monument Valley

▲ Portland Head Light, Maine

▼ Mt Rainier National Park

▼ Castle Geyser, Yellowstone National Park

▲ Double Arch, Utah

▲ Mt Jefferson, Oregon

▼ Green River, Utah

▲ Rialto Beach, Washington

▼ Blue Mesa, in the Petrified Forest of Arizona

Bass Harbor Light on Mount Desert Island, Maine ▶

▲ Cincinatti, Ohio

▲ The Capitol, Washington, D.C.

▼ City Hall, Philadelphia, Pennsylvania

▼ The *Natchez* on the Mississippi, New Orleans

▲ The White House, Washington, D.C.

▲ Walt Disney World, Florida

▼ Mt Rushmore, South Dakota

▼ Miami Beach, Florida

◄ Gateway Arch, St Louis, Missouri

▼ The Washington Memorial

▲ Boston, Massachusetts

76

▲ Canyon de Chelly, Arizona

▲ Mt McKinley, Alaska

▼ Mt Baker, Oregon

▼ The Grand Tetons, Wyoming

▼ Crater Lake and Wizard Island, Oregon

Maroon Lake, Colorado

▼ Hidden Lake, Glacier National Park, Montana

▲ Grand Canyon, Arizona

▼ Niagara Falls, New York

▼ Painted Desert, Arizona

East Mitten and West Mitten in Monument Valley, Arizona ▶

▲ Devastation Trail, Hawaii

▼ Orchids, Hawaii

▼ Glory bush, Hawaii

▼ Waikiki Beach, Oahu, Hawaii

▼ Hawaiian dancer

▼ Church of All Nations, Lihue, Hawaii

▼ Silversword plant, Hawaii

▼ Sea Life Park, Oahu, Hawaii

▲ St Peter's Catholic Church, Hawaii

▼ Hana Highway, Hawaii

▼ Hawaiian beach

▲ Coco Palms Lagoon, Hawaii

▼ Kailua Harbour, Hawaii

83

◄ Honolulu on Oahu, Hawaii

▲ The *Queen Mary* at Long Beach, California

▲ Times Square, New York

▲ Brooklyn Bridge, New York

▼ Manhattan skyline

▼ Central Park, New York

▲ 5th Avenue, New York

▼ Metropolitan Opera House, New York

▲ Mount Vernon, Virginia

▲ Glen Auburn, Natchez, Mississippi

The Court House, Williamsburg, Virginia

▲ Jekyll Island, Georgia

▼ Atlanta, Georgia

▼ Slave houses, South Carolina

▲ Park scene

▼ Fifth Avenue

New York: ▲ Central Park

▼ Lower East Side

▲ The Statue of Liberty

▼ The Plaza Hotel

▼ Prometheus, Rockefeller Center

90

▲ Empire State Building

▼ New York

▼ The Municipal Building

▲ Hansom cabs in Central Park

▼ Fifth Avenue

▲ Manhattan, New York ▶

▲ Brooklyn Bridge

▼ Lower East Sid

New York: ▲ The Chrysler Building

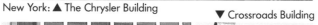
▼ Crossroads Building

▲ New York

▼ Pan Am Building

▼ Helmsley Palac

94

▲ Lower East Side

▲ Liberty Island

▼ Statue of Liberty

ELIZABETH ARDEN

THE
STATUE
OF LIBERTY

Fifth Avenue

▼ Christmas in the Channel Gardens

▼ New York's Chinatown

▲ Dorado Beach Hotel, Puerto Rico

▼ Seven Seas Beach, Puerto Rico

▲ San Juan Cathedral, Puerto Rico

▼ Luquillo, Puerto Rico

▲ Marine life, Puerto Rico

▲ Sports stadium, San Juan, Puerto Rico

▼ Sea turtles, Puerto Rico

▲ Palo Seco, Puerto Rico

▼ Anasco, Puerto Rico

101

▲ Ocho Rios, Jamaica

▼ Limbo dancing, Jamaica

Beach scene, Grenada ▶

102

▲ Paradise Island, Bahamas

▲ Ocho Rios, Jamaica

▼ Sail boats, Jamaica

▼ The Blue Lagoon, Jamaica

▲ Paradise Island Hotel, Bahamas

▼ Nassau Harbour, Bahamas

▲ Nassau, Bahamas

▼ Nassau Beach, Bahama

▼ Cluffs Bay, Barbados

▲ Bridgetown, Barbados ▶

▼ North Beach, Barbados

Colourful dancers, Puerto Vallarta, Mexico

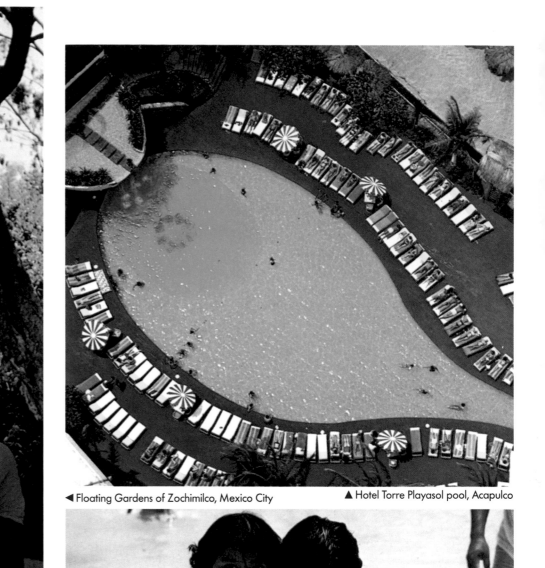

◄ Floating Gardens of Zochimilco, Mexico City　　　▲ Hotel Torre Playasol pool, Acapulco

▲ Turtle riding, Mexico

107

CANADA

▲ Columbia Icefield, Canada

▲ Peggy's Cove, Nova Scotia

▼ Calgary Stampede, Canada

▲ Fort Steele, British Columbia

▼ Gaspé Peninsula, Quebec

▼ Parliament Buildings, Ottawa

▼ Laurentian Region, Quebec

Totem pole, Western Canada

▲ Old Fort Henry, Ontario

▼ Peggy's Cove, Nova Scotia

▼ Fort Edmonton, Alberta

▼ Calgary, Alberta

▼ Chateau Frontenac, Quebec

▲ Muttart Conservatory, Edmonton

▲ Alberta oilfield

▲ Gaspé Peninsula, Quebec

▲ Dinosaur Provincial Park, Alberta

▲ Nova Scotia

▲ Calgary Stampede

▼ Grain silos, Alber

▼ Rural Alberta

112

▲ Totem pole, Western Canada

▼ Parliament Buildings, Victoria, B.C.

▲ R.C.M.P., Calgary

▲ Gaspé Peninsula, Quebec

▲ Alberta farmland

▼ Barkerville, B.C.

▲ The Old City Hall, Toronto, Ontario

Ontario Place, Toronto, Ontario ▶

▲ Cirrus Mountain and Sunwapta Pass in Banff National Park, Alberta

Millbay on Lake Superior, Ontario ▶

◀ Moraine Lake, Alberta

▲ Lake Louise Ski Resort in Banff National Park, Alberta

▲ The Expo Centre, Vancouver, B.C.

The Château Laurier Hotel, Quebec ▶

▼ Near Ballinahinch, Co. Galway

Ashford Castle, Cong, Co. Mayo ▲

▲ Co. Galway

Dublin ▼

▼ Downpatrick Head, Co. Mayo

▲ Co. Galway

Dublin ▼

▲ Kissing the Blarney Stone, Co Cork

▲ Asleagh Falls, Co. Mayo

Relaxation, Co. Donegal ▲

▼ Co. Donegal

▲ Jaunting car, Killarney

Croagh Patrick, Co. Mayo ▲

Ashford Castle, Co. Mayo ▶

▼ Dublin

125

◄ Slyne Head, Co. Galway

Doon Point on the Dingle Peninsula, Co. Kerry ►

▲ The Dingle Peninsula, Co. Kerry

▲ The Dingle Peninsula, Co. Kerry   ▼ Carrick-a-rede, Co. Antrim   ▼ Blarney Castle, Co. Cork   ▼ Jaunting car, Dingle Peninsula, Co. Kerry

▲ Birr Castle, Co. Offaly

▼ The Rock of Cashel, Co. Tipperary

▲ The Dingle Peninsula, Co. Kerry

▼ The White Rocks, Co. Antrim

127

◀ Gortin Glen Forest Park, Co. Tyrone

▲ Powerscourt, Co. Wicklow

▲ The Cliffs of Moher, Co. Clare

Inisheer, Aran Islands ▶

▲ The Four Courts, Dublin

O'Connell Street, Dublin ▶

▲ O'Connell Bridge, Dublin

Scenes from Irish life ▶ ▶

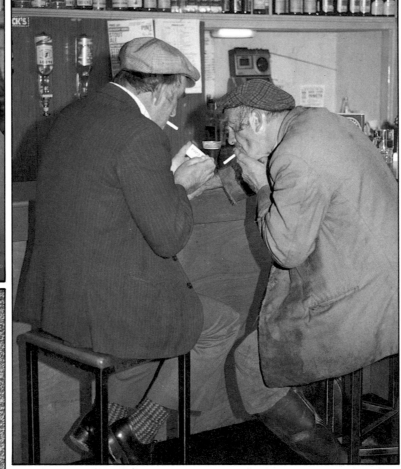

135

London: ▲ City skyline

▼ St Paul's Cathedral

◄ Tower of London

▲ Garter Ceremony, Windsor, Berkshire

▲ Hampton Court Palace

▲ London fog

▲ Post Office Tower

▲ London pageantry

▼ Christmas, Trafalgar Square

The Old Curiosity Shop ▼

The Old Curiosity Shop immortalised by Charles Dickens
Antique and Modern Art

▲ London ceremonial

▼ Regent's Canal

Tower Bridge

London: ▲ County Hall,

The Palace of Westminster ▶

London: ▲ Parliament Square

▲ Chelsea Pensioners in the Royal Hospital, Chelsea

▲ St Paul's Cathedral

▼ Household Cavalry on the Mall

▲ Welsh Guards

▲ Parliament Square

▼ Westminster Abbey

▼ Lambeth Bridge

▼ St James's Park

143

▲ The Palace of Westminster, London ▶

St Paul's Cathedral, London ▶

◄ Oast houses, Kent

▲ The Shambles, Yor

▲ Queen's College, Cambridge

▼ Anne Hathaway's Cottage, Stratford-upon-Avo

▲ Swan Hotel, Lavenham, Suffolk

▼ Thatched cottages, Devon

▲ Bath Abbey, Avon

▼ Lindisfarne Castle, Holy Island

▲ Crummock Water, Lake District

▲ Bodiam Castle, Sussex

▼ Little Moreton Hall, Cheshire

▲ Durdle Door, Dorset

▼ Cricket, Oxfordshir

▲ River Isis, Oxford

▲ Chatsworth House, Derbyshire

▼ King's College, Cambridge

▼ Quay Hill, Lymington, Hants

▼ Cavendish, Suffolk

151

▲ Castle Combe, Wiltshire

▼ Bickleigh, Devon

◀ River Thames, Richmond

▲ Hidcote Manor, West Midlands

▼ Gold Hill, Shaftesbury

▼ Keswick Carles, Cumbria

▲ Magdalen College and the River Thames, Oxford

Blenheim Palace at Woodstock, Oxfordshire ▶

WALES

▲ Newbridge-on-Wye, Powys

▲ Picton Castle, Dyfed

▼ Conwy Castle, Gwynedd

▼ St David's Cathedral, Dyfed

Pembroke Castle, Dyfed ▶

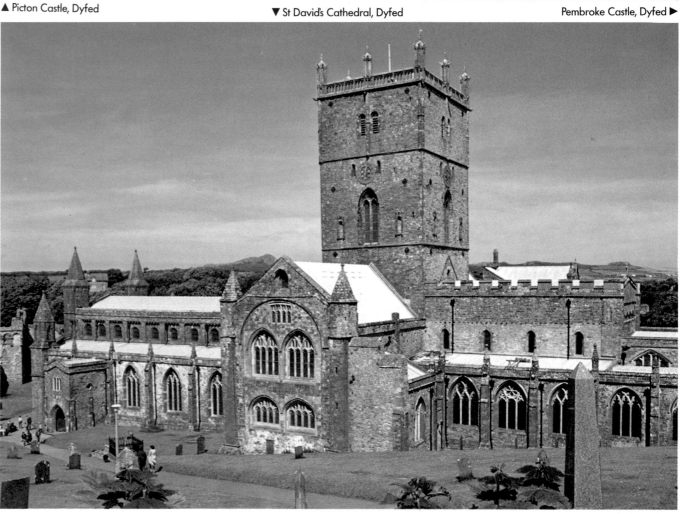

◀ A rushing stream in Gwynedd

SCOTLAND

◄ Balmoral Castle   ▲ St Andrews   ▼ Edinburgh Castle

▲ ▼ Kilchurn Castle, on Loch Awe

▲ John Knox's house, Edinburgh

▲ Dunbeath Castle

▼ Abbotsford

Loch Linnhe in the Highlands ▶

▲ Loch Garry

▲ Loch Leven

▼ Glenfinnan at Loch Shiel

▼ A stag in the Highlands

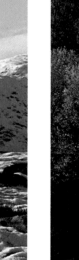

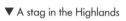
▲ Inverary Castle, Loch Fyne

▼ The Crinan Canal

...snaby Castle, Orkney

▼ A piper

▲ Eilean Donnan Castle, Loch Duich

▼ Abbotsford, the Borders ▼ Eilean Donnan Castle

▲ Loch Leven

▼ A Highland cow

▲ Castle Moil and the harbour of Kyleakin, Isle of Skye

Kilchurn Castle, Strathclyde ▶

SCANDINAVIA

▲ Helsinki, Finland

▲ Riddarholm Church, Sweden

▼ Tivoli Gardens, Copenhagen, Denmark

▲ Kirkehamm, Norway

 Reine, Norway

▲ Amalienborg Palace, Copenhagen, Denmark

▼ Tivoli Gardens, Copenhagen, Denmark

Church at Kerimaki, Finland ▶

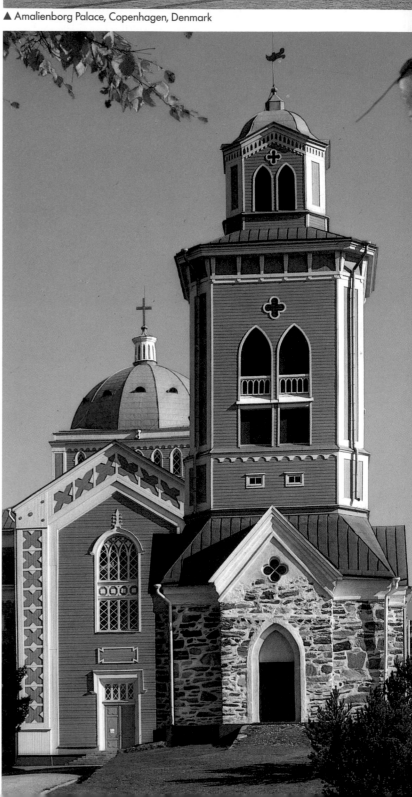

▲ Berne, Switzerland

▲ Chairlifts

▼ The Matterhorn

▼ Aigle Cast

▲ The Matterhorn

Lucerne

▼ Near Interlaken

▲ Murten

▼ Swiss skiing scene

175

▲ Monstein

▼ Graubünden

▼ Mürren

▲ Sleigh riders near Arosa

176

▲ The Water Tower, Lucerne

▼ The Kramgasse, Berne

177

▲ Grossmünster Cathedral, Zurich

▲ The Madonna del Sasso Church, Locarno

▼ Gstaad

178

▲ The harbour of Spiez on Lake Thun

▲ Skiers at Saas-Fee

▼ Château du Chillon, Lake Geneva

◀ Austrian Tyrol ▲ Alpbach ▼ Church at Mosern, near Seefeld

▲ Ober-Gurgl, in the Ötztal Alps

▼ Holidaymakers near Vorarlberg ▲ Typical Austrian village church, and ski resort ▼

▲ The Zillertal

▲ Innsbruck

▼ Berwang

▼ Spanish Riding School, Vienna

182

▲ Heiterwang

▲ Ornamental Gardens, Vienna

▼ Igls, Tyrol

▼ Nassereith

▼ Kitzbühl scene

▲ Nassereith church

▼ Modern Tyrolean church

Pertisau ▶

184

▲ St Wolfgang

▼ Salzburg

▲ Nauders, Tyrol

▼ Sölden, Tyrol

▼ Kitzbühl Alps

▲ Ellmau

▲ Kufstein

▲ The Alcazar, Segovia

▼ Mudejar Pavilion, Seville

▲ Flamenco dancers

▼ Salamanca

◀ The Alhambra, Granada   ▲▼ Plaza de España, Seville

▲ The National Palace Fountains, Barcelona

▲ San Pablo Hospital, Barcelona

▲ Fountains at Montjuich, Barcelona

▲ Royal Palace, Madrid

▲ Consuegra windmills

▲ The Apollo Fountain, Madrid

▲ Spanish roofs and windmills

▲ Palafrugell

▲ Plaza de Espana, Seville

HOLLAND

▲ Bridge over the Herengracht, Amsterdam

▲ Giethoorn

▼ Cheesemaking, near Volendam

▲ Keukenhof Gardens, Lisse

▼ Cycle rental, Amsterdam

▲ Alkmaar cheese market

▼ Montelbaans Tower, Amsterdam

▲ A hand-operated barrel-organ

Amsterdam: ▲ Damrak Harbour

▼ A shop window

▼ The Waals Eilandsgracht

▲ Central Station

▲ The House of Three Canals

▼ A canal dwelling

▼ Damrak Harbour

▲ The Keukenhof Gardens, Lisse

An illuminated bridge on the Reguliersgracht, Amsterdam ▶

▲ The Mint Tower, Amsterdam

▲ Giethoorn

▲ The Magere Brug, Amsterdam

▼ Canal, Amsterdam

▼ Windmill

200

▲ Marken

▲ Lisse

▼ Keukenhof Gardens, Lisse

▼ Sunset over the Zuiderzee

▲ Vineyards, Upper Douro Valley

▼ Port cellars, Douro Valley

Grape harvest ▶

Lisbon

▼ Ageing port, Douro Valley

Basilica da Estrela, Lisbon ▶

▲ Paros

▲ Mykonos

▼ Thirassia

Parthenon, Athens ▶

▼ Corfu Town, Corfu

The mole, Mandraki Harbour, Rhodes

Naoussa, Paros

▼ Paros

▲ 'Venice', Mykonos Town

▼ Corfu Town, Corfu

▲ A thatched windmill above Mykonos town

Mykonos harbour ▶

▲ Parthenon, Athens

▲ Church, Mykonos

▲ Cathedral, Thira

▼ Mykonos

▼ Thirassi

▲ Hydra Harbour, Hydra

▲ The Acropolis, Athens

▼ The harbour, Iraklio, Crete

209

◀ St Mavri Paraportiani Church, Mykonos town

▲ Fishermen, Mykonos harbour

▲ A Corfu sunset

The Parthenon, Athens ▶

GERMANY

▲ Ramsau, near Berchtesgaden

▲ Hamelin

▼ The Rathaus, Memmingen

▼ Münden

▼ Cologne Cathedral

▲ Michelstadt, Hesse

▼ St Columan Church, near Füssen

▲ Flensburg

▼ Bernkastel

▼ The Rathaus, Münden

▲ Heidelberg at night

The Neckar River, Heidelberg ▶

▲ Neuschwanstein Castle

▲ Hamburg

▲ Klein Venedig, Bamberg

▼ Heidelberg

▲ Bernkastel

▼ Monreal, Eife

218

▲ St Pauli District, Hamburg

▲ Brandenburg Gate, Berlin

▼ 'Checkpoint Charlie', Berlin

▼ Alsterpavillon Cafe, Hamburg

▲ Kaiser Wilhelm Memorial Church, West Berlin

The Rathaus, Hamburg ▶

▲ Monschau

▲ Charlottenburg Palace, Berlin

▲ Rothenburg

Punderich ▶

Kitzingen

Traben-Trarbach

▼ Ratzburger Lake

225

▲ Glienicker Bridge, West Berlin

▲ Spandau Citadel, West Berlin

▼ Nymphenburg Castle, Munich

▲ Kaiser Wilhelm Memorial Church, West Berlin

▼ Lünebu

▲ The Lech River at Landsberg

▲ The Brandenburg Gate, from West Berlin

▼ Freiburg im Breisgau

▲ Oktoberfest at Munich

▼ Holstein Gate, Lübeck

225

▲ Lieser

▼ The New Castle, Baden-Baden

▼ Meselbrunn Castle, in the Spessart Mountains

▲ Bernkastel

▼ Baden-Baden

▲ Schloss Besichitizung, near Kunz

▲ The Hesse State Theatre, Wiesbaden

▼ Allemarkstrasse, Hamelin

▲ Runkel Castle and the Lahn River

▲ Poppelsdorfer Castle, Bonn

▼ Freudenberg

229

▲ A ruined castle by the lower Mosel

The Maria Gern Church near Berchtesgaden ▶

▲ Basilica of St Mark

▼ Church of Santa Maria della Salute

Venice: ▲ The Grand Canal

▼ The Rialto Bridge

▲ Campanile and the Piazzetta San Marco

▲ Colourful houses

▲ Face of Coducci's Clock Tower

▲ Sphere on the Dogana da Mar

◄▲▼ Gondoliers

Musician, St Mark's Square

▼ Café in St Mark's Square

233

Venice: ▲ Palazzo Ducale and the campanile

Santa Maria della Salute ▶

◀ Venice: The Church of Santa Maria della Salute

▲ The campanile and Palazzo Ducale, on St Mark's Square

Venice: ▲ The Piazzetta San Marco

▲ The campanile and the Basilica of St Mark

▼ The Clock Tower

▼ Venetian gondolas

e Grand Canal and Santa Maria della Salute

Punta della Dogona da Mar

▲ The Church of San Giorgio Maggiore and the Canale di San Marco

▼ A canal behind St Mark's Square

▼ The Palazzo Ducale

239

▲ Camogli, on the Riviera di Levante

▲ Palazzo Pubblico, Siena

▼ Lake Maggiore

▼ Atrani

▲ Fenis, Valle d'Aosta

▼ Vernazzo, Cinqueterre region

Portofino, Riviera di Levante

▼ Lake Misurina, Dolomite Mountains

▲ A lake near Misurina in the Dolomite Mountains

Livigno, near the Swiss border ▶

▲ Lerici

▼ The Tiber, Rome

▲ Cathedral and Leaning Tower, Pisa

▼ Lake Garda

St Peter's, Rome

▲ Cathedral, Siena

▼ Positano

Overleaf: (left) Portovenere and (right) Portofino

245

◀ The Cathedral and Leaning Tower, Pisa

▲ The Temple Vespasianus and the Temple of Saturne, Rome

Rome: ▲ The Spanish Steps and the Church of Trinita dei Monti

The Fountain of the Moor in the Piazza Navona ▶

Rome: ▲ The National Monument to Victor Emmanuel II

▲ The Spanish Step▪

▼ A statue in the Palazzo della Civilta dei Lavoro

▼ Angel on the Ponte San Angelo

252

▲ The Fountain of Trevi

▼ The Dioscuri and Palazzo Senatorio on the Capitol

▲ Atrani

◀ A statue by the National Monument to Victor Emmanuel II

▼ St Peter's

▼ The Colonnade, St Peter's Square

FRANCE

Paris: ▲ the Basilica of Sacré Coeur

▲ The Arc de Triomphe

▼ Notre Dame

▼ Statue of Victory at the Grand Palais

▼ Folies-Bergère Theatre

Previous pages: (left) Basilica of St Peter, (right) Colosseum, Rome

▲ Palace of Versailles

▲ Parisian park

▼ Louis XIV, Versailles

▼ A game of boules

Diana, Versailles

▼ Rue des Abesses, Montmartre

▼ Gardens of Versailles

257

Paris: ▲ The Arc de Triomphe

A fountain on the Place de la Concorde ▶

▲ The Champs-Elysées

▲▼ Place du Tertre, Montmartre

◄▼► Place du Tertre, Montmartre

Overleaf: (left) Place de la Concorde, (right) Eiffel Tower

260

▲ Notre Dame on the Île de la Cité

▼ The Place de la Concorde

▲ Joan of Arc, Place des Pyramides

▼ Notre Dame

▲ Arc de Triomphe

▲ Paris café

▼ River Seine and Eiffel Tower

▼ Palais de Justice

▼ Street artists

▲ Montmartre, Paris ▶

▲ Azay-le-Rideau, Loire Valley

▼ Château at Sully-sur-Loire

◄ French Riviera

▼ Villefranche, French Riviera

▲ Marseilles

▲ Chateau de Villandry, Loire Valley

▲ Bordeaux region

▼ St Raphael, French Riviera

▼ Resort of La Grande Motte

▼ Château de Saumur

▼ Saint Jean de Luz

269

▲ The Palace of Versailles

Château de Chambord, the Loire Valley ▶

▲ A hotel in Monte Carlo, Monaco

▲ Marseilles

▼ A champagne vineyard

▼ The château of a prosperous vineyard

▼ Cannes

▲ A château

▲ A country house

▼ French fare

▼ A windmill in Picardie

▲ Land near Aix-en-Provence

The Mont-Dore area, Massif Central ▶

▲ Port of Monaco

The Prince's Palace ▶

▲ Castle at Kalmar, Smaland

▲ Rättvik church

▼ Skiing in Jämtland

▼ Gränna, Smaland

▼ Church boat on Lake Siljan

▲ The Old Town, Stockholm

▲ ▼ Sightseeing boats on Riddarfjärden, Stockholm

Royal Palace guard, Stockholm   ▼ Lake Vättern

Overleaf: skiing, Areskutan (left) and Stekenjokk boglands (right)

▲ Jokkmokk, Lappland

▲ Areskutan

▼ Norra Hamngatan, Gothenburg

▼ Skane countryside

▼ Kyrkesund Harbour, Tjörn Island

▼ Windmill, Västergötland

▲ Drottningholm Castle

▲ Duved church

▼ St Peter's Church, Malmö

Läckö Castle, Västergötland

▼ Church boat, Rättvik

▼ Nordiska Museum, Stockholm

◀ St Basil's Cathedral, ▲ Red Square, Moscow. ▼ Troika.

St Saviour's Church, Leningrad ▶

▲ Yad Vashem Memorial, ▼ Dominus Flevit, Independence Menorah ▶

▲ Western Wall, Jerusalem

▼ Bethlehem

▲ Dome of the Rock, Jerusalem

▲ Western Wall, Jerusalem

▲ Shrine of the Book, Jerusalem

▼ Dead Sea

▼ Six Day War Memorial

▼ Monastery of the Cross

▲ West Bank Arabs

▼ Bedouin, Red Sea

▲ Palm Sunday

▼ Western Wall, Jerusalem

▲ ▼ Egyptian tomb paintings

▼ Tomb paintings and sunset, Egypt ▶

▲ Giza pyramid, ▼ Wall painting and nomad, Egypt ▶

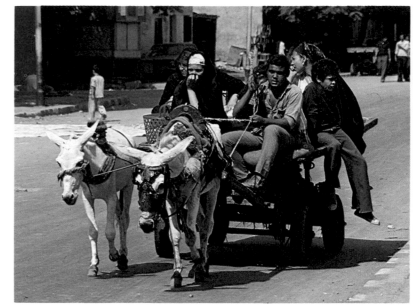

◄▲▼ Egyptian street scenes

▼ Old Cairo skyline

◀ ▲ ▼ Everyday life in Cairo

296 ▲ The Sphinx and pyramid of King Chephren

▲ Pyramid of Cheops

▼ Temple of Luxor

◀ Abu Simbel and ▲ Giza

297

▲ Hyenas

▼ Lion cub

▲ Lion cubs

▼ Cheetahs

▼ Lioness

▼ Buffalo

▲ Elephants

▼ Leopard

▼ Giraffe and zebras

▲ Cheetah

▼ Marabou storks

▲ Elephants

▲ Cheetah

▼ Hippopotamuses

▼ Greater Kudu

▲ Springbok

▲ Cheetah

▼ Lions

▼ Zebra

▼ Leopard

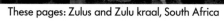

These pages: Zulus and Zulu kraal, South Africa

◄ Table Mountain, Cape Town

▲ The J.G. Strydom Tower, Johannesburg

305

▲ The harbour of Durban

The gardens of the Union Buildings, Pretoria ▶

▲ Diwan-i-Am, in the Red Fort, Agra

▼ Gateway, Jaipur

▲ Agra's fabled Taj Mahal

▲ The Golden Temple of Amritsar

▲ Golden Pavilion of Agra

▼ Typical Islamic non-representational decoration

▲ The Taj Mahal, Agra

▼ Agra

▼ New Delhi and the Red Fort

▲ The Taj Mahal, Agra ▶

311

▲ The tomb of Itmad-ud-Daula, Agra

▲ A pool by the Raj Path, Delhi

▼ Delhi

▼ Delhi

▲ Old Delhi ▼

◀ India Gate, Delhi

▲ The Raj Path, Delhi

▲ The Red Fort, Agra

▼ The Taj Mahal, Agra

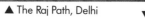▼ The Viceregal Palace, Delhi

315

▲ Pilgrims bathing in the Ganges ▼   ▲ The Ganges at Hardwar   ▼ A teacher at the Kumbu Mela festival   Benares ▶

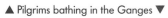

◀ Benares ▼

▲ The Kumba Mela festival, Hardwar

▲ By the Ganges at Hardwar

▼ Burning ghats at Benares

▲ Victoria Memorial, Calcutta

▼ Gomat Raja statue

▲ Dawn ritual, the Ganges

▲ Bombay

▼ Parthasarathi Temple, Madras

▲ The image of Matanga Yaksha, Ellora

The Kailasanatha Temple, Ellora ▶

▲ The palace at Amber, Rajasthan

The Lake Palace Hotel in Udaipur, Rajasthan ▶

▲ The festival of *Holi*

▲ Udaipur

▼ The Tower of Fame, Chittorgarh

▼ A Rajasthani

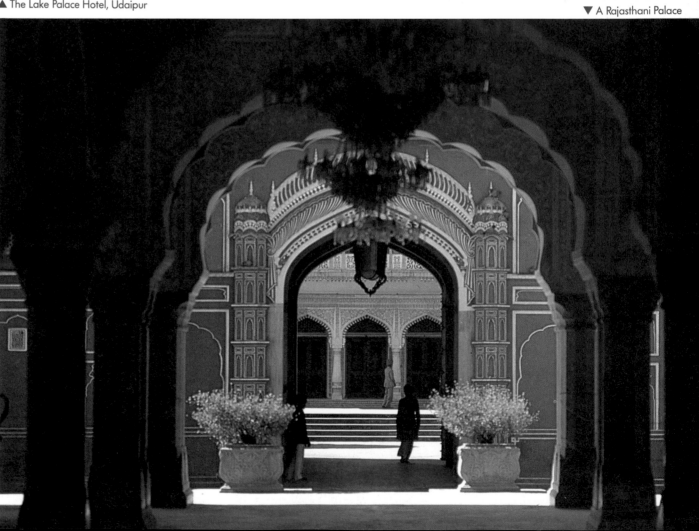

▲ Jaipur

The Palace of the Winds ▶

▲ The Kumba Mela festival, Hardwar ▼

Benares ▶

▲ The Kumba Mela festival, Hardwar ▼

▲ A Royal Procession

▼ Carpet weavers

◀ Terai   ▲ A Nepalese Temple   ▼ The Hima

▲ A Tharus girl of Terai

▲ Fish-tail Mountain

▼ A Buddhist stupa

▼ Nepalese mother and child

333

◀ Nepalese dancers   ▲ A Tibetan-style temple

▼ A market

A well-caparisoned elephant ▶

▲ Kosanji Temple

▼ Cherry Blossom festival

▼ Japanese calligrapher

◀ Garden at Eigen-ji   ▲ Kyoto

▲ Tea ceremony instruction   ▼ Typical farmhouse scene

▲ Sumotori parade

▲ Sumo wrestling

▼ The Bullet train

▼ Seaweed collection, Makuhar

◀ Cherry blossom   ▲ Takamatsu Castle

▲ Mount Fuji   ▼ Traditional Japanese dress

▲ Japanese garden

▲ A garden at Shishendo

▼ Matsue Castle, South Honshu

▼ Imperial Palace, Tokyo

◀ Saimoyo-ji Temple ▼ Kyoto scene ▲ Golden Pavilion, Kyoto

▼ Classic Japanese interior

▲ Hong Kong Harbour

◄▲ Balinese dancers

▼ Driftwood collecting, Bali

▲ Balinese cremation

▲ Hong Kong street scene

▼ Hong Kong market   ▼ Balinese religious festival

◀ Hong Kong　　　▲ ▼ Singapore

◀ Hong Kong Harbour

▲ ▼ street scenes

▲ ▼ Shanghai commune

Landscape near Likiang ▶

▼ Shanghai classroom

▲ Shanghai commune

▲ ▼ Shanghai commune

▲ Huang Ch'iung Yu, Peking

▲ Cave temple, Honan Province

▼ Peking opera

▼ Ch'i Nien Tien, Peking

◄ The Great Wall

▲ Peking department store

▲ Chinese art treasures

▼ Peking

▲ Papua New Guinea

▲ Papua New Guinea

▲ Papua New Guinea

◄▲ Jamaica

▼ Tuvalu

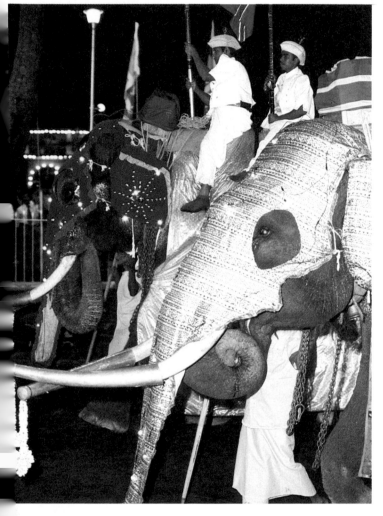

This page: celebratory scenes, Sri Lanka

▲ Kalgoorlie, Western Australia

▼ Perth, Western Australia

▲ ▼ Perth, Western Australia

▲ Ayers Rock

▲ Termite mound, Hamersley Range, Western Australia

▼ The Olgas

Palm Valley Reserve ▶

▲ A beach near Port Douglas, Queensland

355

▲ The Opera House

▼ Harbour Bridge, Sydney

▲ ▼ The Gold Coast, Queensland

356

▲ Brisbane

▲ Canberra

▼ Bronte Beach, Sydney

▼ Brisbane

▲ Tasman Bridge, Tasmania

Sydney Harbour Bridge and Opera House ▶

▲ Port Campbell National Park, Victoria

▲ Sovereign Hill, Ballarat

▼ Melbourne

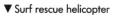
▼ Surf rescue helicopter

▼ Strand Arcade, Sydney

▲ Hobart, Tasmania

▲ Adelaide, S.A.

▼ Yallingup National Park, W.A.

▲ Adelaide, S.A.

▼ Adelaide, South Australia

◄ Norman Bay, Victoria

▲ Squeaky Beach, Victoria

▲ Memorial to Captain Cook, Yeppoon, Qld

▲ Anzac Parade and Parliament Building, Canberra

▼ Beechworth, Victoria

▲ Australian National Gallery, Canberra

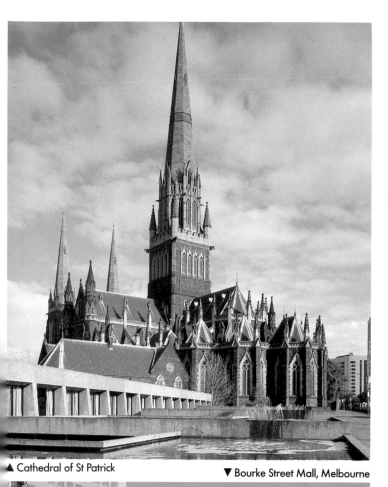
▲ Cathedral of St Patrick

▲ Exhibition Buildings

▼ Bourke Street Mall, Melbourne

▼ The Victorian Arts Centre, Melbourne

◀ Port Campbell National Park, Victoria

▲ St Kilda Road, Melbourne, Victoria

▲ The Olgas, Northern Territory ▶

▲ Fox Glacier

▲ Oriental Bay Marina, Wellington

▲ Parnell Village, Auckland

▼ Black Jack Scenic Reserve, Coromandel Peninsula

▼ Mitre Peak, Fiordland

▲ Westhaven Marina, Auckland

▲ Franz Josef Glacier

▼ Mount Cook

▼ Lake Wakatipu from Deer Park Heights

▼ River Avon, Christchurch

▲ Milford Sound, New Zealand

The Ngauruhoe volcano, Tongariro National Park ▶

◀ Mount Egmont in the Taranaki Region

▲ Anaura Bay, near Gisborne

Sandfly Bay, on the Otago Peninsula ▶

▲ The Fletcher Bridge spanning the Franz Josef Glacier

INDEX

AFRICA
African wildlife 298, 299, 300, 301
Kenya 34
Mount Kilimanjaro, Tanzania 57
Tississat Falls, Blue Nile 60
Victoria Falls 60

AUSTRALIA
Adelaide, South Australia 361, 365
Anzac Parade, Canberra 366
Australian National Gallery,
  Canberra 366
Ayers Rock 353
Beechworth, Victoria 366
Bourke Street Mall, Melbourne
  367
Brisbane 357
Bronte Beach, Sydney 357
Canberra 357
Captain Cook Memorial, Yeppoon,
  Queensland 366
Exhibition Buildings, Melbourne
  367
Gold Coast, Queensland 356, 364
Hammersley Range, Western
  Australia 353
Harbour Bridge, Sydney, 356, 359
Heron Island, Queensland 355
Hobart, Tasmania 361
Kalgoorlie, Western Australia 352
Melbourne 360
Norman Bay, Victoria 362
Olgas 353, 370, 371
Opera House, Sydney 356, 359
Palm Valley Reserve 353
Parliament Building, Canberra 366
Perth, Western Australia 352
Port Campbell National Park,
  Victoria 360, 368
Sovereign Hill, Ballarat 360
Squeaky Beach, Victoria 363
St Kilda Road, Melbourne 369
St Patrick's Cathedral, Melbourne
  367
Strand Arcade, Sydney 360
Tasman Bridge, Tasmania 358
Victorian Arts Centre, Melbourne
  367
Yallingup National Park, Western
  Australia 361

AUSTRIA
Alpbach 180
Berwang 182
Ellmau 186
Heiterwang 183
Igls, Tyrol 183
Innsbruck 182
Kitzbühl 183
Kitzbühl Alps 186
Kufstein 187
Mosern 180
Nassereith 183, 184
Nauders, Tyrol 186
Ober-Gurgl 181
Ornamental Gardens, Vienna 183
Pertisau 184
Salzburg 185
Spanish Riding School, Vienna
  182
St Wolfgang 185
Sölden, Tyrol 186
Tyrol 180
Zillertal 182

CANADA
Alberta 112, 113
Banff National Park, Alberta 116
Barkerville, British Columbia 113
British Columbia 34
Calgary, Alberta 109
Calgary Stampede, Alberta 108,
  112
Château Frontenac, Quebec 109
Château Laurier Hotel, Quebec
  121
Columbia Icefield 108
Dinosaur Provincial Park, Alberta
  112
Expo Centre, Vancouver 120
Fort Edmonton, Alberta 109
Fort Steele, British Columbia 108
Gaspé Peninsula, Quebec 108,
  112, 113
Lake Louise Ski Resort, Alberta
  119
Lake Superior, Ontario 117
Laurentian Region, Quebec 108
Lion's Gate Bridge, Vancouver
  111
Moraine Lake, Alberta 118
Muttart Conservatory, Edmonton
  112

Nova Scotia 112
Old City Hall, Toronto 114
Old Fort Henry, Ontario 109
Ontario Place, Toronto 115
Parliament Buildings, Ottawa 108
Parliament Buildings, Victoria 113
Peggy's Cove, Nova Scotia 108,
  109
Vancouver, British Columbia 110

CARIBBEAN
Blue Lagoon, Jamaica 103
Bridgetown, Barbados 105
Cluffs Bay, Barbados 105
Grenada 102
Jamaica 102, 103, 350
Nassau Beach, Bahamas 104
Nassau Harbour, Bahamas 104
North Beach, Barbados 105
Ocho Rios, Jamaica 102, 103
Paradise Island, Bahamas 103,
  104

CHINA
Cave temple, Honan Province 348
Ch'i Nien Tien, Peking 348
Great Wall 349
Huang Ch'iung Yu, Peking 348
Likiang 346
Peking 349
Shanghai 346, 347

DENMARK
Amalienborg Palace, Copenhagen
  173
Tivoli Gardens, Copenhagen 172,
  173

EGYPT
Abu Simbel 297
Cairo 294, 295
Egypt, general 50, 292
Giza 293, 297
Pyramid of Cheops 296
Pyramid of King Chephren 296
Sphinx 296
Temple of Luxor 296

ENGLAND
Anne Hathaway's Cottage,
  Stratford-upon Avon 146

Bath Abbey, Avon 147
Bickleigh, Devon 157
Blenheim Palace, Oxfordshire 158
Bodiam Castle, Sussex 150
Canterbury Cathedral, Canterbury
  149
Castle Combe, Wiltshire 157
Cavendish, Suffolk 151
Chatsworth House, Derbyshire 151
County Hall, London 138
Crummock Water, Lake District
  150
Devon 147
Durdle Door, Dorset 150
Gold Hill, Shaftesbury 157
Grasmere, Cumbria 155
Hampton Court Palace, 136
Henley Regatta 52
Hidcote Manor, West Midlands
  157
High Force, Cumbria 154
Hurstbourne Tarrant, Hampshire
  152
Keswick Carles, Cumbria 157
King's College, Cambridge 151
Lambeth Bridge, London 141
Land's End, Cornwall 153
Lavenham, Suffolk 147
Leigh-on-Sea, Essex, England 43
Lindisfarne Castle, Holy Island
  147
Little Moreton Hall, Cheshire 150
Lymington, Hampshire 151
Magdalen College, Oxford 158
Mall, London 140
Nelson's Column, London 47
Oasthouses, Kent 146
Old Curiosity Shop, London 137
Oxford Street, London 38
Oxfordshire 150
Palace of Westminster, London 50,
  139, 142, 143
Parliament Square, London 140
Parliament Square, London 141
Piccadilly Circus, London 46
Post Office Tower, London 137
Queens College, Cambridge 146
Regents Canal, London 137
River Isis, Oxford 151
River Thames, Richmond 156
Royal Hospital, Chelsea, London
  140

Shambles, York 146
St George's Chapel, Windsor 144
St James's Park, London 141
St Paul's Cathedral, London 136,
    140, 145
Tower Bridge, London 137
Tower of London, London 136
Trafalgar Square, London 137
Waterloo Bridge, London 39
Westminster Abbey, London 141
Windsor Castle, Windsor 148

FINLAND
Helsinki 172
Kerimaki 173

FRANCE
Arc de Triomphe, Paris 256, 258,
    265
Azay-le-Rideau 268
Cannes 272
Champs Elysées, Paris 260
Château de Chambord 271
Château de Saumur 269
Château de Villandry 269
Eiffel Tower, Paris 51, 263, 265
Folies Bergère, Paris 256
La Grande Motte 269
Marseilles 268, 272
Montmartre, Paris 257, 260, 261,
    266, 267
Notre Dame, Paris 256, 264
Palais de Justice, Paris 265
Place de la Concorde, Paris 259,
    262, 264
Place des Pyramides, Paris 264
River Seine 265
Sacré Coeur, Paris 256
Saint Jean de Luz 269
St Raphael 269
Statue of Victory, Paris 256
Sully-sur-Loire 268
Versailles 257, 270
Villefranche 268

GERMANY
Baden-Baden 228
Bernkastel 215, 218
Bernkastel 228
Brandenburg Gate, Berlin 219, 225
Charlottenburg Palace, Berlin 222

'Checkpoint Charlie', Berlin 219
Cologne Cathedral 214
Flensburg 215
Freiburg im Breisgau 225
Freudenberg 229
Glienicker Bridge, West Berlin
    224
Hamburg 218, 219
Hamelin 214, 229
Heidelberg 216, 217, 218
Hesse State Theatre, Wiesbaden
    229
Holstein Gate, Lübeck 225
Kaiser Wilhelm Memorial Church,
    West Berlin 220, 224
Kitzingen 223
Klein Venedig, Bamberg 218
Lech River, Landsberg 225
Lieser 228
Lüneburg 224
Maria Gern Church, near Berchtes-
    gaden 231
Meselbrunn Castle 228
Michelstadt, Hesse 215
Monreal, Eifel 218
Monschau 222
Monschau, Germany 33
Mosel River 230
Mosel River, Kochem 226
Munich Oktoberfest 225
Münden 214
Neckar River, Heidelberg 217
Neuschwanstein Castle 218
New Castle, Baden-Baden 228
Nymphenburg Castle, Munich 224
Poppelsdorfer Castle, Bonn 229
Punderich 222
Ramsau 214
Rathaus, Hamburg 221
Rathaus, Memmingen 214
Rathaus, Münden 215
Ratzburger Lake 223
Rothenburg 222
Runkel Castle 229
Schloss Besichtizung 229
Spandau Citadel, West Berlin 224
St Columan Church, near Füssen
    215
Traben-Trarbach 223

GREECE
Acropolis, Athens 209
Corfu 212
Corfu Town, Corfu 204, 205
Hydra Harbour, Hydra 209
Iraklio Harbour, Crete 209
Mandraki Harbour, Rhodes 205
Mykonos 38, 204, 208
Mykonos Harbour 207, 211
Mykonos Town 205, 206
Naoussa, Paros 205
Paros 204, 205
Parthenon, Athens 204, 208, 213
Thira 208
Thirassia 204, 208
St Mavri Paraportiani Church,
    Mykonos Town 210

HOLLAND
Alkmaar Cheese Market 34, 195
Amsterdam 200
Central Station, Amsterdam 197
Damrak Harbour, Amsterdam 196,
    197
Giethoorn 194, 200
Herengracht, Amsterdam 194
House of Three Canals 197
Keukenhof Gardens, Lisse 43,195,
    198, 201
Lisse 201
Magere Brug, Amsterdam 200
Marken 201
Mint Tower, Amsterdam 199
Montelbaans Tower, Amsterdam
    195
Reguliersgracht, Amsterdam 198
Waals Eilandsgracht, Amsterdam
    196
Zuiderzee 201

HONG KONG, BALI AND
SINGAPORE
Bali 342, 343,
Hong Kong 35, 343, 344, 345
Hong Kong Harbour 34, 47, 342,
    345
Rice fields, Bali 50
Sanur Beach, Bali 39
Singapore 344

INDIA
Agra 310
Amber palace, Rajasthan 324
Benares 317, 318, 319, 330
Bombay 321
Delhi 312, 313
Diwa-i-Am, Agra 308
Ellora 322, 323
Golden Pavilion of Agra 309
Golden Temple, Amritsar 309
Gomat Raja statue 320
Hardwar 319, 330, 331
India Gate, Delhi 314
Itmad-ud-Daula tomb, Agra 312
Jaipur 308, 328
Lake Palace Hotel, Udaipur 325,
    327
New Delhi 310
Palace of the Winds 329
Parthasarathi Temple, Madras 321
Raj Path, Delhi 315
Red Fort, Agra 315
River Ganges 316, 319, 320
Taj Mahal 53, 308, 310, 311, 315
Tower of Fame, Chittorgarh 326
Udaipur 326
Viceregal Palace, Delhi 315
Victoria Memorial, Calcutta 320

IRELAND
Ashford Castle, Co. Mayo 122,
    123
Asleagh Falls, Co. Mayo 123
Birr Castle, Co. Offaly 127
Blarney Castle, Co. Cork 126
Blarney Stone, Co. Cork 123
Carrick-a-rede, Co. Antrim 126
Cliffs of Moher, Co. Clare 130
Co. Donegal 123
Co. Galway 122
Croagh Patrick, Co. Mayo 123
Dingle Peninsula, Co. Kerry 125,
    126, 127
Downpatrick Head, co. Mayo 122
Dublin 122, 123
Four Courts, Dublin 132
Gortin Glen Forest Park, Co.
    Tyrone 128
Inisheer, Aran Islands 131
Ireland 134, 135
Killarney 123

O'Connell Bridge, Dublin 132
O'Connell Street, Dublin 133
Powerscourt, Co. Wicklow 129
Rock of Cashel, Co. Tipperary 127
Slyne Head, Co. Galway 124
White Rocks, Co. Antrim 127

ISRAEL
Dead Sea 290
Dome of the Rock, Jerusalem 289
Dominus Flevit, Jerusalem 288
Independence Menorah 288
Monastery of the Cross, Jerusalem 290
Red Sea 291
Shrine of the Book, Jerusalem 290
Six Day War Memorial 290
Western Wall, Jerusalem 52, 289, 290
Yad Vashem Memorial 288

ITALY
Atrani 240
Atrani 253
Basilica of St Mark, Venice 232, 238
Camogli 240
Campanile, Venice 233, 234, 237, 238
Canale di San Marco, Venice 239
Capitol, Rome 253
Cathedral and Leaning Tower, Pisa 244, 248
Cathedral, Siena 245
Coducci's Clock Tower, Venice 233, 238
Colisseum, Rome 255
Dogana da Mar sphere, Venice 233
Dolomites 242
Fenis 241
Grand Canal, Venice 232, 239
Lake Garda 244
Lake Maggiore 240
Lake Misurina 241
Lerici 244
Livigno 243
National Monument, Rome 252, 253
Palazzo Ducale, Venice 234, 237, 239
Palazzo Pubblico, Siena 240

Piazza Navona, Rome 251
Piazzeta San Marco, Venice 238
Portofino 241
Portofino 247
Portovenere 246
Positano 245
Punta della Dogona da Mar 239
Rialto Bridge, Venice 44, 232
San Giorgio Maggiore, Venice 239
Santa Maria della Salute, Venice 53, 232, 235, 236, 239
Sella Massif 241
Spanish Steps, Rome 250, 252
St Mark's Square, Venice 233
St Peter's, Rome 245, 253, 254
St Peter's Square 253
Temple of Saturne, Rome 249
Temple Vespasianus, Rome 249
Tiber, Rome 244
Trevi Fountain 253
Trinita dei Monti, Rome 250
Venice 39, 51
Vernazzo 241

JAPAN
Bullet Train 338
Eigen-ji garden 337
Golden Pavilion, Kyoto 341
Imperial Palace, Tokyo 340
Kosanji Temple 336
Kyoto 337
Matsue Castle, South Honshu 340
Mount Fuji 339
Saimoyo-ji Temple 341
Shishendo garden 340
Takamatsu Castle 339

MEXICO
Bullfight, Mexico City 44
Fiesta, Mexico 45
Floating Gardens of Zochimilco, Mexico City 107
Hotel Torre Playasol, Acapulco 107
Mexico 35, 106

MONACO
Monte Carlo 272, 276, 277

NEPAL
Dhaulargiri Glacier 56

Fish-tail Mountain 333
Guaesh Himal mountains 57
Himalayas 332
Mount Everest, Himalayas 56, 57
Nepal, general 331, 334, 335
Terai 332

NEW ZEALAND
Anaura Bay 377
Black Jack Scenic Reserve, Coromandel Peninsula 372
Fox Glacier 372
Franz Josef Glacier 373, 380
Lake Wakatipu 373
Milford Sound 374, 378
Mitre Peak, Fiordland 372
Mount Cook 373
Mount Egmont 376
Mount Ngauruhoe 375
Oriental Bay Marina, Wellington 372

NORWAY
Briksdalbreen glacier 56
Kirkehamm 172
Reine 173

PAPUA NEW GUINEA 350

PORTUGAL
Basilica da Estrela, Lisbon 203
Douro Valley 202, 203
Lisbon 203

RUSSIA
Red Square, Moscow 286
St Basil's Cathedral, Moscow 286
St Saviour's Church, Leningrad 287

SCOTLAND
Abbotsford 165, 169
Balmoral Castle 164
Castle Moil, Isle of Skye 170
Crinan Canal 168
Dunbeath Castle 165
Edinburgh Castle 164
Eilean Donnan Castle 169
Firth of Forth suspension bridge 46
Glenfinnan 168
Inverary Castle, Loch Fyne 168

John Knox's house, Edinburgh 165
Kilchurn Castle, Loch Awe 165, 171
Kyleakin Harbour, Isle of Skye 170
Loch Garry 168
Loch Leven 168, 169
Loch Linnhe, Highlands 167
River Beathach, Glen Orchy 166
St Andrews 164
Yesnaby Castle, Orkney 169

SOUTH AFRICA
Durban Harbour 306
J.G. Strydom Tower, Johannesburg 305
Table Mountain, Cape Town 304
Union Buildings gardens, Pretoria 307
Zulus and kraal 302, 303

SOUTH AMERICA
Brasilia, Brazil 42
Iguaçu Falls 61
Machu Picchu, Peru 61
Rio de Janeiro, Brazil 60

SPAIN
Alcazar, Segovia 188
Alhambra, Granada 189
Apollo Fountain, Madrid 191
Canary Islands 51
Consuegra 191
Montjuich Fountains, Barcelona 190
Mudejar Pavilion, Seville 188
National Palace Fountains, Barcelona 190
Palafrugell 192
Plaza de España, Seville 189, 193
Royal Palace, Madrid 190
Salamanca 188
San Pablo Hospital, Barcelona 190

SRI LANKA 351

SWEDEN
Areskutan 280, 282
Drottningholm Castle 283
Duved church 283